Grammar Dimensions

Book 1B   **Second Edition**

Form, Meaning, and Use

Grammar Dimensions

BOOK 1B   SECOND EDITION

Form, Meaning, and Use

Diane Larsen-Freeman
Series Director

Victoria Badalamenti   Carolyn Henner Stanchina
LaGuardia Community College   Queens College
City University of New York

Listening Activities in this text were developed by the editorial team
at Heinle & Heinle Publishers.

Heinle & Heinle Publishers

I(T)P   An International Thomson Publishing Company

Pacific Grove • Albany • Bonn • Boston • Cincinnati • Detroit • London
Madrid • Melbourne • Mexico City • New York • Paris
San Francisco • Tokyo • Toronto • Washington

The publication of *Grammar Dimensions Book One*, Second Edition, was directed by members of the Newbury House ESL/EFL Team at Heinle & Heinle:

Erik Gundersen, Editorial Director
Bruno R. Paul, Market Development Director
Kristin M. Thalheimer, Production Services Coordinator
Nancy Mann Jordan, Developmental Editor
Stanley J. Galek, Vice President and Publisher

Also participating in the publication of this program were:

Project Manager/Desktop Pagination: Thompson Steele Production Services
Production Editor: Maryellen Eschmann Killeen
Manufacturing Coordinator: Mary Beth Hennebury
Associate Editor: Ken Pratt
Associate Market Development Director: Mary Sutton
Photo/Video Specialist: Jonathan Stark
Media Services Coordinator: Jerry Christopher
Interior Designer: Greta Sibley
Illustrators: Lyle Miller and Walter King
Photo Coordinator: Philippe Heckly
Cover Designer: Gina Petti, Rotunda Design
Cover Photo: Rowena Otremba, The Fringe

Heinle & Heinle Publishers is a division of International Thomson Publishing, Inc.

Manufactured in the United States of America

Library of Congress Cataloging-in-Publication Data

Badalamenti, Victoria.
  Grammar dimensions: Form, meaning, and use / Victoria Badalamenti, Carolyn Henner Stanchina; Diane Larsen-Freeman, series director.
    p. cm.
  Includes index.
  ISBN 0-8384-7163-3
  1. English language—Textbooks for foreign speakers. 2. English language—Grammar—Problems, exercises, etc. I. Henner Stanchina, Carolyn. II. Larsen-Freeman, Diane. III. Title.
PE 1128, B233 1997
428.2'4—dc21
                               96-48584
                                  CIP

10 9 8 7 6 5 4 3

A Special Thanks

The series director, authors, and publisher would like to thank the following individuals who offered many helpful insights and suggestions for change throughout the development of *Grammar Dimensions, Second Edition.*

Jane Berger
Solano Community College, California

Mary Bottega
San Jose State University

Mary Brooks
Eastern Washington University

Christina Broucqsault
California State Polytechnic University

José Carmona
Hudson Community College

Susan Carnell
University of Texas at Arlington

Susana Christie
San Diego State University

Diana Christopher
Georgetown University

Gwendolyn Cooper
Rutgers University

Sue Cozzarelli
EF International, San Diego

Catherine Crystal
Laney College, California

Kevin Cross
University of San Francisco

Julie Damron
Interlink at Valparaiso University, Indiana

Glen Deckert
Eastern Michigan University

Eric Dwyer
University of Texas at Austin

Ann Eubank
Jefferson Community College

Alice Fine
UCLA Extension

Alicia Going
The English Language Study Center, Oregon

Molly Gould
University of Delaware

Maren M. Hargis
San Diego Mesa College

Mary Herbert
University of California, Davis Extension

Jane Hilbert
ELS Language Center, Florida International University

Eli Hinkel
Xavier University

Kathy Hitchcox
International English Institute, Fresno

Joyce Hutchings
Georgetown University

Heather Jeddy
Northern Virginia Community College

Judi Keen
University of California, Davis, and Sacramento City College

Karli Kelber
American Language Institute,
New York University

Anne Kornfeld
LaGuardia Community College

Kay Longmire
Interlink at Valparaiso University, Indiana

Robin Longshaw
Rhode Island School of Design

Bernadette McGlynn
ELS Language Center,
St. Joseph's University

Billy McGowan
Aspect International, Boston

Margaret Mehran
Queens College

Richard Moore
University of Washington

Karen Moreno
Teikyo Post University, Connecticut

Gino Muzzetti
Santa Rosa Junior College, California

Mary Nance-Tager
LaGuardia Community College,
City University of New York

Karen O'Neill
San Jose State University

Mary O'Neal
Northern Virginia Community College

Nancy Pagliara
Northern Virginia Community College

Keith Pharis
Southern Illinois University

Amy Parker
ELS Language Center, San Francisco

Margene Petersen
ELS Language Center, Philadelphia

Nancy Pfingstag
University of North Carolina, Charlotte

Sally Prieto
Grand Rapids Community College

India Plough
Michigan State University

Mostafa Rahbar
University of Tennessee at Knoxville

Dudley Reynolds
Indiana University

Ann Salzman
University of Illinois at Urbana-Champaign

Jennifer Schmidt
San Francisco State University

Cynthia Schuemann
Miami-Dade Community College

Jennifer Schultz
Golden Gate University, California

Mary Beth Selbo
Wright College, City Colleges of Chicago

Stephen Sheeran
Bishop's University, Lenoxville, Quebec

Kathy Sherak
San Francisco State University

Keith Smith
ELS Language Center, San Francisco

Helen Solorzano
Northeastern University

Book 1B Contents

(see page xii for Book 1A Contents)

UNIT 13   DIRECT AND INDIRECT OBJECTS, OBJECT PRONOUNS

187

Focus 1 >>>>Direct Objects (Form/Meaning)   189
Focus 2 >>>>Direct Object Pronouns (Form/Use)   190
Focus 3 >>>>Indirect Objects (Form/Meaning)   193
Focus 4 >>>>Position of the Indirect Object (Form)   195
Focus 5 >>>>Position of New Information (Use)   197
Focus 6 >>>>Verbs that Do Not Omit *To* with Indirect Objects (Form)   200

UNIT 14   CAN, KNOW HOW TO, BE ABLE TO, AND/BUT/SO/OR

205

Focus 1 >>>>*Can* (Form/Meaning)   206
Focus 2 >>>>Questions with *Can* (Form)   208
Focus 3 >>>>Asking for Help with English (Use)   210
Focus 4 >>>>Expressing Ability: *Can*, *Know How to*, and *Be Able to* (Form/Meaning/Use)   211
Focus 5 >>>>Sentence Connectors: *And/But/So/Or* (Form/Meaning)   214

UNIT 15   PRESENT PROGRESSIVE TENSE

219

Focus 1 >>>>Present Progressive: Affirmative Statements (Form/Meaning/Use)   221
Focus 2 >>>>Spelling of Verbs Ending in *-ing* (Form)   223
Focus 3 >>>>Present Progressive: Negative Statements (Form)   225
Focus 4 >>>>Choosing Simple Present or Present Progressive (Use)   227

Focus 5 >>>>Verbs Not Usually Used in the Progressive (Meaning)   229

Focus 6 >>>>Present Progressive: *Yes/No* Questions and Short Answers (Form)   232

Focus 7 >>>>Present Progressive: *Wh-* Questions (Form)   234

UNIT 16   ADJECTIVE PHRASES

Another, The Other, Other(s), The Other(s), Intensifiers   239

Focus 1 >>>>Adjective Phrases (Form/Meaning)   241

Focus 2 >>>>Questions with *Which* (Form/Meaning)   245

Focus 3 >>>>*Another, The Other, Other(s), The Other(s)* (Form/Meaning)   247

Focus 4 >>>>Intensifiers (Form/Meaning)   250

UNIT 17   PAST TENSE OF BE

257

Focus 1 >>>>Past Tense of B*e*: Affirmative Statements (Form)   259

Focus 2 >>>>Past Tense of B*e*: Negative Statements (Form)   261

Focus 3 >>>>*Yes/No* Questions and Short Answers with B*e* in the Simple Past (Form)   263

Focus 4 >>>>*Wh-* Questions with B*e* (Form)   265

UNIT 18   PAST TENSE

269

Focus 1 >>>>Spelling of Regular Past-Tense Verbs (Form)   271

Focus 2 >>>>Pronunciation of the *-ed* Ending (Form)   274

Focus 3 >>>>Irregular Past-Tense Verbs: Affirmative Statements (Form)   277

Focus 4 >>>>Time Expressions (Form/Meaning)   281

Focus 5 >>>>Past Tense: Negative Statements (Form)   283

Focus 6 >>>>Past Tense: *Yes/No* Questions and Short Answers (Form)   284

Focus 7 >>>>Past Tense: *Wh-* Questions (Form)   286

UNIT 19   REFLEXIVE PRONOUNS, RECIPROCAL PRONOUN, EACH OTHER

293

Focus 1 >>>>Reflexive Pronouns (Form)   295
Focus 2 >>>>Verbs Commonly Used with Reflexive Pronouns/By + Reflexive Pronoun (Meaning/Use)   296
Focus 3 >>>>Reciprocal Pronoun: *Each Other* (Meaning)   298

UNIT 20   FUTURE TIME

Will and Be Going To; May and Might   **303**

Focus 1 >>>>Talking about Future Time (Meaning/Use)   305
Focus 2 >>>>*Will* (Form)   306
Focus 3 >>>>*Be Going To* (Form)   310
Focus 4 >>>>Time Expressions (Form/Meaning)   314
Focus 5 >>>>Talking about Future Intentions or Plans (Use)   318
Focus 6 >>>>*May* and *Might* (Form/Meaning)   320

UNIT 21   PHRASAL VERBS

325

Focus 1 >>>>Phrasal Verbs (Form/Meaning)   327
Focus 2 >>>>Phrasal Verbs (Meaning/Use)   328
Focus 3 >>>>Separable and Inseparable Phrasal Verbs (Form)   330
Focus 4 >>>>Common Separable and Inseparable Phrasal Verbs (Meaning)   332
Focus 5 >>>>Common Phrasal Verbs without Objects (Form/Meaning)   336

UNIT 22   COMPARISON WITH ADJECTIVES

341

Focus 1 >>>>Comparative Form of Adjectives (Form)   343
Focus 2 >>>>Questions with Comparative Adjectives (Form)   348
Focus 3 >>>>Expressing Similarities and Differences with As . . . As (Meaning)   350
Focus 4 >>>>Making Polite Comparisons (Use)   351

UNIT 23   COMPARISON WITH ADVERBS

357

Focus 1 >>>>Comparative Forms of Adverbs (Form/Use)   359

Focus 2 >>>>Expressing Similarities and Differences (Form/Meaning)   361

Focus 3 >>>>Questions with *How* (Form/Meaning)   364

UNIT 24   SUPERLATIVES

371

Focus 1 >>>>Superlatives (Meaning)   373

Focus 2 >>>>Regular and Irregular Superlative Forms (Form)   374

Focus 3 >>>>*One of the* + Superlative + Plural Noun (Meaning/Use)   380

UNIT 25   FACTUAL CONDITIONAL

If   **385**

Focus 1 >>>>Expressing Facts (Form/Meaning)   387

Focus 2 >>>>Expressing Habitual Relationships (Meaning)   388

Focus 3 >>>>Order of Clauses in Factual Conditionals (Form/Use)   391

APPENDICES

A-1

Appendix 1   Forming Verb Tenses   A-1
  A.   *Be*: Present Tense
  B.   *Be*: Past Tense
  C.   Simple Present
  D.   Present Progressive
  E.   Simple Past
  F.   Future Tense with *Will*
  G.   Future Tense with *Be Going To*
  H.   *Can/Might/May*
  I.   *Be Able To*

Appendix 2   Spelling Rules   A-4
  A.   Plural Nouns
  B.   Simple Present: Third Person Singular
  C.   Present Progressive
  D.   Simple Past of Regular Verbs

Appendix 3   Pronunciation Rules   A-6
    A.   Regular Plural Nouns
    B.   Simple Present Tense: Third Person Singular
    C.   Simple Past Tense of Regular Verbs

Appendix 4   Time Expressions   A-7
    A.   Simple Present
    B.   Present Progressive
    C.   Past
    D.   Future

Appendix 5   Pronouns   A-9
    A.   Subject Pronouns
    B.   Object Pronouns
    C.   Demonstrative Pronouns
    D.   Possessive Pronouns
    E.   Reflexive Pronouns
    F.   Reciprocal Pronoun

Appendix 6   Possessives   A-11
    A.   Possessive Nouns
    B.   Possessive Determiners
    C.   Possessive Pronouns

Appendix 7   Comparisons with Adjectives and Adverbs   A-12
    A.   Comparative Form
    B.   Superlative Form
    C.   A/As

Appendix 8   Past-Tense Forms of Common Irregular Verbs   A-13

ANSWER KEY
        (for puzzles and problems only)   **AK-1**

EXERCISES
        (second parts)   **E-1**

CREDITS
        C-1

INDEX
        I-1

1A Contents

UNIT 1   THE VERB BE

Affirmative Statements, Subject Pronouns   **1**

Focus 1 >>>>Be: Affirmative Statements (Form)   3

Focus 2 >>>>Subject Pronouns with Be (Form/Meaning/Use)   5

Focus 3 >>>>Contractions with Be (Form)   9

Focus 4 >>>>Introductions and Greetings (Use)   11

UNIT 2   THE VERB BE

Yes/No Questions, Be + Adjective, Negative Statements   **15**

Focus 1 >>>>Be: Yes/No Questions and Short Answers (Form)   17

Focus 2 >>>>Be + Adjective (Form)   19

Focus 3 >>>>Be: Negative Statements and Contractions (Form/Use)   23

UNIT 3   THE VERB BE

Wh-Question Words, Prepositions of Location   **29**

Focus 1 >>>>Wh-Question Words with Be (Form/Meaning)   31

Focus 2 >>>>How to Ask Questions about English (Use)   34

Focus 3 >>>>Using It to Talk about the Weather (Use)   35

Focus 4 >>>>Using It to Talk about Time (Use)   37

Focus 5 >>>>Prepositions of Location (Form/Meaning)   40

UNIT 4   NOUNS

Count and Noncount Nouns, Be + Adjective + Noun   **47**

Focus 1 >>>>Count Nouns and Noncount Nouns (Form/Meaning)   49

Focus 2 >>>>A/An with Singular Count Nouns (Form)   50

Focus 3 >>>>Spelling of Regular Plural Count Nouns (Form)   54

Focus 4 >>>>Regular Plural Nouns: Pronunciation of Final -s and -es (Form)   56

Focus 5 >>>>Irregular Plural Nouns (Form)   58

Focus 6 >>>>Count and Noncount Nouns (Form)   59

Focus 7 >>>>How Much Is/How Much Are . . . ? (Form/Use)   61

Focus 8 >>>>Be + Adjective + Noun (Form)   62

UNIT 5   THE VERB HAVE

Affirmative and Negative Statements, Questions and Short Answers; *Some/Any*   **65**

Focus 1 >>>>Have and Has: Affirmative Statements (Form/Meaning)   67

Focus 2 >>>>Have: Negative Statements and Contractions (Form)   68

Focus 3 >>>>Have: Yes/No Questions and Short Answers (Form)   69

Focus 4 >>>>Some/Any (Form)   73

Focus 5 >>>>Asking for Something Politely (Use)   75

Focus 6 >>>>Using Have to Describe People (Use)   76

UNIT 6   THIS/THAT/THESE/THOSE POSSESSIVES

79

Focus 1 >>>>This, These, That, Those (Form/Meaning)   81

Focus 2 >>>>Asking What Things Are (Form/Use)   83

Focus 3 >>>>Possessive Nouns (Form)   85

Focus 4 >>>>Possessive Adjectives, Pronouns (Form)   88

Focus 5 >>>>Questions with Whose (Form/Meaning)   90

UNIT 7   THERE IS/THERE ARE

A/An versus The   **93**

Focus 1 >>>>There + Be (Meaning/Use)   95

Focus 2 >>>>There Is/There Are (Form)   96

Focus 3 >>>>There Isn't/There Aren't/There's No/There Are No (Form)   98

Focus 4 >>>>Yes/No Questions with There Is/There Are (Form)   100

Focus 5 >>>>Choosing A/An or The (Use)   102

UNIT 8   SIMPLE PRESENT TENSE

Affirmative and Negative Statements, Time Expressions: *Like/Want/Need*   **109**

Focus 1 >>>>Talking about Habits and Routines (Use)   111

Focus 2 >>>>Simple Present Tense: Affirmative Statements (Form)   111

Focus 3 >>>>Third Person Singular: Spelling and Pronunciation
               (Form)   113

Focus 4 >>>>Frequency and Time Expressions (Meaning)   116

Focus 5 >>>>Frequency and Time Expressions (Form)   117

Focus 6 >>>>Simple Present: Negative Statements (Form)   119

Focus 7 >>>>Talking about Things that Are Always True (Use)   120

Focus 8 >>>>*Like*, *Want*, *Need* (Form/Meaning)   122

UNIT 9   SIMPLE PRESENT TENSE

Yes/No Questions, Adverbs of Frequency, *Wh*-Questions   129

Focus 1 >>>>Simple Present: *Yes/No* Questions (Form)   131

Focus 2 >>>>Adverbs of Frequency (Meaning)   135

Focus 3 >>>>Position of Adverbs of Frequency (Form/Use)   137

Focus 4 >>>>Simple Present: *Wh*-Questions (Form/Meaning)   139

Focus 5 >>>>*Wh*- Questions with *Who/Whom* (Form/Meaning/Use)   141

Focus 6 >>>>Getting Information about English (Use)   143

UNIT 10   IMPERATIVES AND PREPOSITIONS OF DIRECTION

147

Focus 1 >>>>Imperatives: Affirmative and Negative (Form)   149

Focus 2 >>>>Uses of Imperatives (Use)   150

Focus 3 >>>>Using Imperatives Appropriately (Use)   153

Focus 4 >>>>Prepositions of Direction: *To, Away, From, On* (*to*), *Off* (*of*), *In* (*to*),
               Out (*of*) (Meaning)   154

Focus 5 >>>>Prepositions of Direction: *Up, Down, Across, Along, Around, Over,*
               Through, Past (Meaning)   156

Focus 6 >>>>Giving Directions (Use)   157

UNIT 11   QUANTIFIERS

161

Focus 1 >>>>Review of Count and Noncount Nouns (Form)   163

Focus 2 >>>>Quantifiers (Form/Meaning)   164

Focus 3 >>>>A *Few/Few, A Little/Little* (Meaning)   168

Focus 4 >>>>Questions with *How Many* and *How Much* (Form)   169

Focus 5 >>>>Measure Words (Meaning)   171

UNIT 12   ADVERBS OF MANNER

177

Focus 1 >>>>Adverbs of Manner (Form/Meaning)   179

Focus 2 >>>>Spelling of Adverbs of Manner (Form)   180

Focus 3 >>>>Talking about a Person or an Action (Use)   184

DIRECT AND INDIRECT OBJECTS,
UNIT 13   OBJECT PRONOUNS

187

Focus 1 >>>>Direct Objects (Form/Meaning)   189

Focus 2 >>>>Direct Object Pronouns (Form/Use)   190

Focus 3 >>>>Indirect Objects (Form/Meaning)   193

Focus 4 >>>>Position of the Indirect Object (Form)   195

Focus 5 >>>>Position of New Information (Use)   197

Focus 6 >>>>Verbs that Do Not Omit *To* with Indirect Objects (Form)   200

APPENDICES

A-1

Appendix 1   Forming Verb Tenses   A-1
    A. *Be*: Present Tense
    B. *Be*: Past Tense
    C. Simple Present
    D. Present Progressive
    E. Simple Past
    F. Future Tense with *Will*
    G. Future Tense with *Be Going To*
    H. *Can/Might/May*
    I. *Be Able To*

Appendix 2   Spelling Rules   A-4
    A. Plural Nouns
    B. Simple Present: Third Person Singular
    C. Present Progressive

D. Simple Past of Regular Verbs

Appendix 3   Pronunciation Rules   A-6
A. Regular Plural Nouns
B. Simple Present Tense: Third Person Singular
C. Simple Past Tense of Regular Verbs

Appendix 4   Time Expressions   A-7
A. Simple Present
B. Present Progressive
C. Past
D. Future

Appendix 5   Pronouns   A-9
A. Subject Pronouns
B. Object Pronouns
C. Demonstrative Pronouns
D. Possessive Pronouns
E. Reflexive Pronouns
F. Reciprocal Pronoun

Appendix 6   Possessives   A-11
A. Possessive Nouns
B. Possessive Determiners
C. Possessive Pronouns

Appendix 7   Comparisons with Adjectives and Adverbs   A-12
A. Comparative Form
B. Superlative Form
C. A/As

Appendix 8   Past-Tense Forms of Common Irregular Verbs   A-13

ANSWER KEY

(for puzzles and problems only)   AK-1

EXERCISES

(second parts)   E-1

CREDITS

C-1

INDEX

I-1

From the Series Editor

To the Teacher

ABOUT THE SERIES

Grammar Dimensions, Second Edition is a comprehensive and dynamic, four-level series designed to introduce English-as-a-second or foreign language students to the form, meaning, and use of English grammatical structures with a communicative orientation. The series has been designed to meet the needs of students from the beginning to advanced levels and includes the following:

- *Grammar Dimensions, Book 1* ....beginning/high beginning
- *Grammar Dimensions, Book 2* ....intermediate
- *Grammar Dimensions, Book 3* ....high intermediate
- *Grammar Dimensions, Book 4* ....advanced

The textbooks are supplemented by workbooks, cassettes, instructor's manuals with tests, and a CD-ROM entitled *Grammar 3D*.

THE STORY OF GRAMMAR DIMENSIONS

Everywhere I went teachers would ask me, "What is the role of grammar in a communicative approach?" These teachers recognized the importance of teaching grammar, but they associated grammar with form and communication with meaning, and thus could not see how the two easily fit together.

Grammar Dimensions was created to help teachers and students appreciate the fact that grammar is not just about form. While grammar does indeed involve form, in order to communicate, language users also need to know what the forms mean and when to use them appropriately. In fact, it is sometimes learning the meaning or appropriate use of a particular grammar structure that represents the greatest long-term learning challenge for students, not learning to form it. For instance, learning when it is appropriate to use the present perfect tense instead of the past tense, or being able to use two-word or phrasal verbs meaningfully represent formidable learning challenges for ESL students.

The three dimensions of form, meaning and use can be depicted in a pie chart with their interrelationship illustrated by the three arrows:

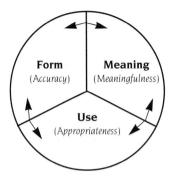

Helping students learn to use grammatical structures accurately, meaningfully, and appropriately is the fundamental goal of *Grammar Dimensions*. It is a goal consistent with the goal of helping students to communicate meaningfully in English, and one that recognizes the undeniable interdependence of grammar and communication.

ABOUT THE BOOKS

The books have been designed to allow teachers to tailor their syllabi for different groups of students. Some teachers have told us that they prefer to teach the units in a different order from that of the book. Teachers should feel free to do so or only to teach part of one unit and then return to do another part at a later time. Since the acquisition process is not a linear one (students do not completely master one structure before moving on to tackle another), teachers can construct syllabi which permit a recycling of material that causes their students difficulty. Of course, some teachers and students would rather use the book more conventionally, as well, by working their way through the units chronologically.

To allow for this possibility, some thought has been given to the sequencing of units within a book. The units have been ordered following different principles depending upon the level of the book. In Book 1, where students are introduced (or reintroduced in the case of false beginners) to basic sentence and subsentence grammatical structures and grammatical forms associated with semantic notions such as time and place, the units have been sequenced following conventional linguistic grading, building from one structure to the next. In Book 2, basic sentence and subsentence grammatical structures are dealt with once again. In addition, Book 2 also introduces language forms that support certain social functions such as making requests and seeking permission. At this level, units that share certain features have been clustered together. No more than three or four units are clustered at one time, however, in order to provide for some variety of focus. Although the four skills are dealt with in all of the books, the listening and speaking skills are especially prominent in Books 1 and 2.

Clustering 2-3 units that address related topics has been done for levels three and four as well. Book 3 deals with grammatical structures that ESL/EFL students often find challenging, such as the use of infinitives and gerunds. It also employs a discourse orientation when dealing with structures such as verb tenses and articles. Students learn how to use grammar structures accurately within contexts above the level of the single sentence. Book 4 deals with grammatical forms that are especially needed for academic and technical writing. It reveals to students the subtleties of certain grammatical structures and how they contribute to cohesion in discourse. Both books highlight the reading and writing skills and target structures for which students at these levels can benefit from special guidance in order to avoid their learning plateauing and their errors fossilizing.

ABOUT THE UNITS

Within a unit, the grammar structure is introduced to students within a communicative orientation. First, students have an opportunity to produce the target grammatical structures in a meaningful opening task. Thus, the grammar is contextualized and students are introduced to its meaning and use prior to any treatment of its form. Next, a series of alternating focus boxes and exercises presents students with the relevant form, meaning, and use facts concerning the target structure and provides practice with each. Finally, communication activities conclude each unit where students can more freely express themselves using the target grammar for communicative purposes. The following elaborates on this format.

Opening Task

In addition to providing a context for the meaningful use of the target grammar structures, the opening task serves several other purposes:

1. The tasks are motivating. Teachers tell us that students find the problem solving enjoyable and somewhat challenging.

2. Moreover, doing the task should activate the knowledge that students do have and help them recognize the need to learn the target structures they have not yet acquired.

3. Students' performance provides teachers with useful diagnostic information about where students' particular learning challenges lie. Thus, teachers can select material within a unit that has the most relevance for their students' learning needs.

Knowing their students' learning challenges helps teachers use their limited time more effectively. For instance, it may be the case that the students already know the target structure, in which case the unit may be skipped. It might also be that only the meaning or use of a particular structure is causing most students difficulty, in which case the focus boxes that deal with form issues can be ignored. Teachers are encouraged to see the book as a resource from which they can select units or parts of units that best meet their students' needs. (See the Instructor's Manual for tips on how to do this.)

Focus Boxes

The facts concerning the target structures are displayed in boxes clearly identified by the dimension(s) they address—form, meaning, or use. Each rule or explanation is preceded by examples. The examples, rules, and explanations are all arrayed in chart form for easy reference. Because the learning challenge presented by the three dimensions of language is not equal for all structures (for instance, some structures present more of a form-based challenge; for others the challenge is learning what the structures mean or when or why to use them), the number and foci of boxes differ from one unit to another.

Exercises

It is important to point out that it is not sufficient for students to know the rules or facts concerning these three dimensions. Thus, in *Grammar Dimensions*, we strive to have students develop the skill of "grammaring"—the ability to use structures accurately, meaningfully, and appropriately. To this end, the exercises are varied, thematically coherent, but purposeful. Often, students are asked to do something personally meaningful (e.g., students might be asked to register some opinion or to explain why they chose the answer that they did).

Activities

Located at the end of each unit, the communicative activities (purple pages) are designed to help students realize the communicative value of the grammar they are learning. As a complement to the meaningful task that opened the unit, grammar and communication are again practiced in tandem. Teachers, or students, may select from the ones offered those that they feel will be most enjoyable and beneficial.

NEW FEATURES IN THE SECOND EDITION

Teachers who have taught with *Grammar Dimensions* will note that the basic philosophy and approach to teaching grammar have not changed from the first edition. We believe they are still sound linguistically and pedagogically, and users of the first edition have confirmed this. However, our series users have also requested several new features, and modifications of others, and we have carefully woven these into this second edition:

1. One new feature that series users will notice is the incorporation of listening. Each unit has at least one activity in which students are asked to listen to a taped segment and respond in some way that involves the target structures.

2. A second new feature is the inclusion of a quiz after every unit to help teachers assess what students have learned from the unit. These 15-minute quizzes are available for duplication from the Instructor's Manuals.

3. Another change we have implemented is to streamline the grammar explanations and make them more user-friendly. You will notice that grammar terms are consistently labeled in the most straightforward and common manner. Also, note that, in each focus box, examples are consistently outlined on the left and explanations on the right to enhance clarity.

4. In response to user feedback, we have limited the texts to 25 units each. As was mentioned above, the material is meant to be used selectively, not comprehensively; still, some users preferred that the books have fewer units to begin with, and we agree that a reduced scope of grammatical topics in each book will help both teachers and students focus more successfully on their greatest learning challenges.

5. To honor the multiplicity of learning styles in the classroom and to capitalize on the dynamism of emerging technologies, we have developed a CD-ROM component called *Grammar* 3D to complement the *Grammar Dimensions* print materials. A wealth of exciting exercises and activities in *Grammar* 3D review and expand upon the lessons presented in the textbooks.

In all these ways, it is our hope that this series will provide teachers with the means to create, along with their students, learning opportunities that are tailored to students' needs, are enjoyable, and will maximize everyone's learning.

Diane Larsen-Freeman
School for International Training

OTHER COMPONENTS

In addition to the student text, each level of *Grammar Dimensions* includes the following components:

Audio Cassette

The audio cassette contains the listenings from the communicative activities (purple pages) in the student text.

An icon ✍ indicates which activities use the audio cassette.

Workbook

The Workbook provides additional exercises for each grammar point presented in the student text. Many of the workbook exercises are specially designed to help students prepare for the TOEFL® (Test of English as a Foreign Language).

Instructor's Manual

The Instructor's Manual contains:

- an introduction to philosophical background of the series
- general teaching guidelines
- unit-by-unit teaching notes
- student text answer key
- workbook answer key
- tapescript
- tests for each unit
- test answer key

CD-ROM

Grammar 3D is an ideal supplement to *Grammar Dimensions*. It provides comprehensive instruction and practice in 34 of the key grammar structures found in the text series.

Grammar 3D is appropriate for high-beginning to advanced students, and allows students to progress at their own pace. Students can access each grammar category at 3 or 4 levels of difficulty. They can then move to a lower level if they need basic review, or to a higher level for additional challenge.

An instructional "help page" allows students to access grammar explanations before they begin an exercise, or at any place within an exercise. Instruction is also provided through feedback that helps students understand their errors and guides them toward correct answers.

An icon indicates which focus boxes are supported by exercises in *Grammar* 3D.

To the Student

All grammar structures have a form, a meaning, and a use. We can show this with a pie chart:

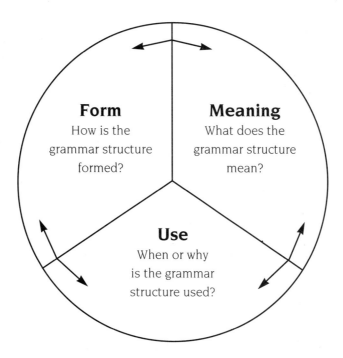

Often you will find that you know the answer to one or more of these questions, but not to all of them, for a particular grammar structure. This book has been written to help you learn answers to these questions for the major grammar structures of English. More importantly, it gives you practice with the answers so that you can develop your ability to use English grammar structures accurately, meaningfully, and appropriately.

At the beginning of each unit, you will be asked to work on an opening task. The task will introduce you to the grammar structures to be studied in the unit. However, it is not important at this point that you think about grammar. You should just do the task as well as you can.

In the next section of the unit are focus boxes and exercises. You will see that the boxes are labeled with FORM, MEANING, USE, or a combination of these, corresponding to the three parts of the pie chart. In each focus box is information that answers one or more of the questions in the pie. Along with the focus box are exercises that should help you put into practice what you have studied.

The last section of each unit contains communicative activities. Hopefully, you will enjoy doing these and at the same time receive further practice using the grammar structures in meaningful ways.

By working on the opening task, studying the focus boxes, doing the exercises, and engaging in the activities, you will develop greater knowledge of English grammar and skill in using it. I also believe you will enjoy the learning experience along the way.

Diane Larsen-Freeman
School for International Training

Acknowledgments

Series Director Acknowledgments

This edition would not have come about if it had not been for the enthusiastic response of teachers and students using the first edition. I am very grateful for the reception *Grammar Dimensions* has been given. By the same token, I want to give special thanks to those users who accepted our invitation to let us know how to better meet their needs with this second edition.

I am grateful for all the authors' efforts as well. To be a teacher, and at the same time a writer, is a difficult balance to achieve. So is being an innovative creator of materials, and yet, a team player. They have met these challenges exceedingly well in my opinion.

Then, too, the Heinle & Heinle team has been impressive. I am grateful for the leadership exercised first by Dave Lee, and later by Erik Gundersen. I also appreciate all the support from Ken Mattsson, Ken Pratt, Kristin Thalheimer, John McHugh, Bruno Paul, and Mary Sutton. Deserving special mention are Jean Bernard Johnston, and above all, Nancy Jordan, who never lost the vision while they attended to the detail with good humor and professionalism.

I have also benefited from the counsel of Marianne Celce-Murcia, consultant for this project, and my friend.

Finally, I wish to thank my family members, Elliott, Brent, and Gavin, for not once asking the (negative yes-no) question that must have occurred to them countless times: "Haven't you finished yet?"

Author Acknowledgments

This book is dedicated to Joel, Melanie, and Michele, who stood steadfastly by, tolerating all the moods and missed moments, as we reeled through this revision process. Their stamina was a great source of strength. This book also stands as an affirmation of the power of friendship; one solid enough to withstand the unspeakable frustrations and pressures of this process.

We are deeply grateful to Diane Larsen-Freeman for her patient guidance and supportive ear. Her intervention, on many occasions, allowed us to preserve the nature and original intent of this text.

We wish to extend our sincere thanks to the women at Thompson Steele Production Services, especially Marcia Croyle who, in the crunch, gave so generously of her time to try to set things right, and even saw the light regarding task-based, communicative grammar!

We also wish to thank both our ESL students at the City University of New York, and our Methods students at Queens College and The New School For Social Research, for their insights.

Finally, we credit Nancy Mann Jordan for her own personal vision and uncompromising efforts in bringing this project to fruition.

UNIT 13

Direct and Indirect Objects, Direct and Indirect Object Pronouns

Giving Gifts

You need to give a gift to the people on your list below. Look at the gifts you have and decide which gift you want to give to each person.

Gifts

A. Camera

B. Flowers

C. Toaster

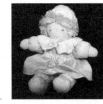

D. Doll

E. Earrings

F. Running Shoes

G. Compact Disc Player

People

1. a single thirty-five-year-old athletic male friend
2. your sixty-three-year-old grandmother
3. your friend's four-year-old daughter
4. an artistic twenty-seven-year-old friend
5. your mother
6. your music-loving boyfriend/girlfriend
7. a newlywed couple

I want to give ~~them~~ them a toaster

FOCUS 1 >>>>>>>>>>>>>>> **FORM/MEANING**

Direct Objects

EXAMPLES			EXPLANATIONS
Subject	**Verb**	**Direct Object**	
(a) My friend	sings.		Some sentences have only a subject and a verb.
(b) He	loves	music.	Some sentences have a subject, a verb, and an object.
(c) He	buys	compact discs.	A direct object answers the question "What?" *Compact discs* is the direct object.
(d) He	loves	the Beatles.	A direct object also can answer the question "Who(m)?" *The Beatles* is the direct object.

EXERCISE 1

Underline the direct object in each sentence below.

EXAMPLE: My friend loves <u>sports</u>.

1. My grandmother loves flowers. She always has fresh flowers on the dining room table.

2. Andrea and Bob have a new home.

3. My mother adores jewelry.

4. My friend's daughter has a doll collection. She owns ten different dolls.

5. Akiko takes beautiful pictures.

6. My friend enjoys classical music. She prefers Mozart.

7. In my family, we always celebrate our birthdays together.

Direct Object Pronouns

EXAMPLES	EXPLANATIONS
Subject **Verb** **Direct Object** **(a)** My mother loves my father. **(b)** My mother loves him.	The direct object can also be a pronoun.
(c) My mother loves **my father.** She thinks about **him** all the time. **(d)** My father loves **my mother.** He thinks about **her** all the time.	Object pronouns refer to a noun that comes before. In (c), *him* refers to "my father." In (d), *her* refers to "my mother."

SUBJECT	VERB	OBJECT PRONOUN	SUBJECT	VERB	OBJECT PRONOUN
I	am				me.
You	are				you.
He	is				him.
She	is	a good person.	She	loves	her.
It	is				it.
We	are				us.
You	are				you.
They	are				them.

EXERCISE 2

Fill in the correct subject or object pronouns.

1. My grandmother is a very special person. (a) _____She_____ has a vegetable garden in her backyard. (b) _____She_____ plants tomatoes, cucumbers, eggplant, leeks and carrots. She picks (c) _____them_____ fresh every day. We love her fresh vegetables. (d) _____They_____ taste delicious. We eat (e) _____them_____ in salads and soup. Her vegetable garden gives (f) _____us_____ great pleasure.

2. Mariela and Juan are newlyweds. (a) _____they_____ have a new home, and
   (b) _____they_____ really love (c) _____it_____. Their appliances are
   on order, but they don't have (d) _____them_____ yet, so Mariela and Juan
   have a lot of work to do. He helps (e) _____her_____ with the cooking. She
   helps (f) _____him_____ with the laundry.

3. Sally: Billy, do you like heavy metal music?

   Billy: (a) _____I_____ (b) love _____it_____!

   Sally: Really? I hate heavy metal. (c) _____It_____ bothers
   (d) _____me_____. I hate all that noise.

EXERCISE 3

This is a story about three people in a love triangle. Maggie has a steady boyfriend, Ted. She also has a male friend, Jim. Read the text below. Cross out the incorrect pronouns and write the correct pronouns above them.

Maggie

Jim

Ted

Maggie loves her boyfriend, Ted. She also likes Jim. (1) Jim works with ~~she~~ *her*.

(2) She sees he *him* every day. (3) She sometimes invites he *him* to dinner. (4) She likes to
talk with he *him*. (5) Maggie doesn't love Jim, but Jim loves she *her*. (6) Jim thinks about
she *her* all the time. Jim knows about Ted, but Ted doesn't know about Jim. Ted is very
jealous. (7) So, Maggie can't tell he *him* about Jim. (8) Maggie doesn't want to leave he *him*.
But she cares for both Ted and Jim. She doesn't know what to do. (9) She doesn't
want to hurt they *them*. She says to herself, "What's wrong with me? (10) Ted loves I *me* and
I love he *him*. (11) Jim is my friend and I like he *him*. So what can I do?"

Ted finds out about Jim. He talks to Maggie on the phone late one night. Fill in the correct object pronouns.

1. **Ted:** Hello, Maggie. Do you remember (a) _me_____?

   Maggie: Of course, I remember (b) _____, Ted. You're my boyfriend!

2. **Ted:** I know about Jim, Maggie.

   Maggie: What? You know about (a) _____?

3. **Ted:** That's right, Maggie. I know everything about (a) _____.

   Maggie: How do you know?

   Ted: John—your secretary—told me. I meet (b) _____ for lunch sometimes. He knows about (c) _____ and Jim.

4. **Ted:** Jim can't come between (a) _____, Maggie.

   Maggie: I know, Ted. Don't worry. I don't love (b) _____.

   We're just friends.

   Ted: Do you love (c) _____?

   Maggie: Of course, I love (d) _____, Ted. I want to marry (e) _____.

5. **Ted:** You can't see (a) _____ so much, Maggie.

   Maggie: Ted, please trust (b) _____.

Ask your partner questions with *how often*. Your partner answers with object pronouns.

   EXAMPLE: You: How often do you call your parents? *9. I'm going to the grocery shopping on friday.*

   Your Partner: I call them every week.

1. clean your room?
2. do your laundry? *I wash*
3. see your dentist? *I see my dentist twice a year* *2 lần*
4. buy the newspaper?
5. cut your nails?

6. wash your hair?
7. visit your friends?
8. drink coffee?
9. do the grocery shopping?
10. watch the news?

2/ I wash clother once a week.

5. I cut my nails once a week.
6. I wash my hair every day. tôi tắm mỗi ngày.
7. I visit my friends on Sunday.

Indirect Objects

EXAMPLES				EXPLANATIONS
Subject	**Verb**	**Direct Object**	**Indirect Object**	
(a) I	want to give	the toaster	to **the newlyweds.**	Some sentences have two objects: a direct object and an indirect object. *The toaster* is the direct object. It tells **what** I want to give. *The newlyweds* is the indirect object. It tells to **whom** I give the toaster.
(b) I	buy	flowers	for **my grand-mother.**	*My grandmother* is the indirect object. It tells for **whom** I buy flowers.
(c) I	want to give	the toaster	to **the newlyweds.**	The indirect object can be a noun or a pronoun.
(d) I	want to give	the toaster	to **them.**	

EXAMPLES	EXPLANATIONS
(e) I fix the car **for** my grandmother.	**For and To** *For* tells us one person does the action to help or please another person.
(f) I give earrings **to** my mother.	*To* tells us about direction of the action: The earrings go from you to your mother.

Write sentences telling what you want to give to each of the people in the Opening Task. Underline the direct object and circle the indirect object. Then tell why you want to give that item to that person.

EXAMPLE: I want to give <u>the toaster</u> to the (newlyweds.) They have a new home and don't have any appliances.

New Year's Resolutions. Every January 1st, North Americans decide to change their lives and do things differently. Read the resolutions below. Change each underlined noun to a pronoun. Then add the information in parentheses.

EXAMPLE: Every year, I give <u>my father</u> a tie. (golf clubs)

This year, I want to give him golf clubs.

1. Used car salesman:

   I always sell <u>my customers</u> bad cars. (good cars)

   This year, I want to sell them good cars.

2. Child away at college:

   I always to write to <u>my parents</u> once a month. (once a week)

   This year, I want to write them once a week.

3. People with money problems:

   Every year, the bank sends (<u>my husband and me</u>) us a big credit card bill. (a very small bill)

   This year, I want the bank to sends us a very small.

4. Boyfriend:

   I usually buy <u>my girlfriend</u> flowers for her birthday. (a diamond ring)

   This year, I want to buy her a diamond ring.

5. Teenager:

   Sometimes I lie to <u>my mother</u>. (tell the truth)

   This year, I want to . . . tell her the truth.

6. Mother:

   I never have time to read to <u>my children</u> at night. (every night)

   This year, I want to read them every night

7. Student:

I always give my homework to <u>the teacher</u> late. (on time)

This semester, I want to .give *her on time.*

8. Friend:

Every year, I lend money to <u>you and your brother</u>. (lend money)

This year, I don't want to .*lend you money.*

Now say three things you want to do differently this year.

FOCUS 4 >>>>>>>>>>>>>>>>>>>>>>>>>>>> **FORM**

Position of the Indirect Object

All verbs that take indirect objects can <u>follow</u> Pattern A.

Say day

Pattern A

SUBJECT	VERB	DIRECT OBJECT	INDIRECT OBJECT
(a) I	give	presents	to my mother on her birthday.
(b) I	give	presents	to her.
(c) I	give	them	to her.
(d) We	have	a party	for our twin daughters on their birthday.
(e) We	have	a party	for them.
(f) We	have	it	for them.

Some of these verbs also follow Pattern B. In Pattern B, put the indirect object before the direct object. Do not use *to* or *for*.

Pattern B

SUBJECT	VERB	INDIRECT OBJECT	DIRECT OBJECT
(g) People	send	their friends	birthday cards.
(h) People	send	them	birthday cards.
(i) I	make	my friends	birthday cakes.
(j) I	make	them	birthday cakes.

NOTE: Do not put an indirect object pronoun before a direct object pronoun.

I make my friend a cake.

I make her a cake.

NOT: I make her it.

Verbs that follow both Pattern A and B

give	send	pass	mail	make	do (a favor)
write	bring	read	offer	buy	find
show	hand	lend	pay	bake	get
tell	sell	teach	throw	cook	

EXERCISE 8

Work with a partner and make sentences about North American customs with the words below.

BIRTH: When a baby is born:

1. mother /flowers /the /to /give /friends

   Friends give flowers to the mother.

2. cigars /gives /friends /father /his /the *or The father gives his*

3. send /and /parents /friends /family /to /birth /announcements /their /the

4. baby /family /friends /gifts /the /buy /and

5. make /for /grandmothers /sweaters /new /the /baby

6. grandfathers /for /toys /make /baby /the

7. child /the /the /parents /everything /give

196   Unit 13

ENGAGEMENT/MARRIAGE: When a couple gets engaged or married:

8. diamond / man / a / woman / the / gives / ring / the / to / sometimes

9. friends / couple / an / party / the / for / have / engagement

10. gifts / woman / give / friends / at a party / the

11. at the wedding / to / couple / gifts / give / guests / the

DEATH: When someone dies:

12. send / family / some / flowers / people / the

13. people / special cards / the / send / family / to

14. some / to / give / people / money / charities

15. some / food / for / family / bring / people / the

FOCUS 5 ➤➤➤➤➤➤➤➤➤➤➤➤➤➤➤➤➤➤➤➤➤➤➤➤ **USE**

Position of New Information

New information in a sentence comes at the end. You can write a sentence in two different ways. Both are correct, but the emphasis is different.

EXAMPLES	EXPLANATIONS
(a) Whom do you give earrings to? I usually give earrings to **my mother.**	The emphasis is on **who(m).** *My mother* is the new information.
(b) What do you usually give your mother? I usually give my mother **earrings.**	The emphasis is on **what.** *Earrings* is the new information.

EXERCISE 9

Answer the following question. The new information is in parentheses ( ).

EXAMPLES: Who(m) do you usually give presents to at Christmas? (my family)

I usually give presents to my family.

What do you usually give your father? (a good book)

I usually give him a good book.

Direct and Indirect Objects, Direct and Indirect Object Pronouns **197**

1. Who(m) do you want to give a present to at work? (three of my co-workers)

2. What do you usually give your parents for their anniversary? (tickets to a play)

3. Who(m) do you tell jokes to? (my friend) *charge her,*

4. What do you sometimes send your sister? (some new recipes)

5. Does she teach English to your brother or sister? (my brother)
   She is teacher English to my brother.

6. Which story do you usually read to your little sister—"Cinderella" or "Snow White"? ("Cinderella") *Cinderella to my sister.*

7. Who(m) do you need to mail the application to? (the admissions office)

8. What do you usually buy for your son on his birthday? (compact discs)
   I usually buy him compact discs.

EXERCISE 10

Choose the best sentence.

EXAMPLE: You are waiting for a friend in front of a restaurant.

You do not have your watch. You want to know the time.

You see someone coming. You ask him:

(a) Could you please tell me the time?

(b) Could you please tell the time to me?

1. You are alone at a restaurant. You finish your meal. You see the waiter. You ask him:

   (a) Could you please give the check to me?

   (b) Could you please give me the check?

2. You are celebrating someone's birthday with a group of friends. You finish your meal. You want to be sure you pay the check. You tell the waiter:

   (a) Please give the check to me.

   (b) Please give me the check.

3. What do your children usually do for you on Mother's Day?

   (a) They usually serve breakfast in bed to me.

   (b) They usually serve me breakfast in bed.

4. You are at a friend's house for dinner. The food needs salt. You say:

   (a) Please pass me the salt.

   (b) Please pass the salt to me.

5. You realize you don't have any money on you for the bus. You ask a friend:

   (a) Could you lend a dollar to me?

   x (b) Could you lend me a dollar?
   ~ borrow

6. You are in class. It is very noisy. You say to a classmate:

   x (a) Do me a favor. Please close the door.

   x (b) Do a favor for me. Please close the door.

7. Why does your class look so sad on Mondays?

   x (a) because our teacher gives us a lot of homework.

   (b) because our teacher gives a lot of homework to us.

8. You are speaking to the Director of the English Language Institute. You want to apply to the City University. You have the application form in your hand.

   Director: x (a) Please send the application form to the City University.

           (b) Please send the City University the application form.

9. You come home from the supermarket. Your car is full of groceries. You need help. You say to your roommate:

   (a) Can you please give a hand to me?

   x (b) Can you please give me a hand?

10. There are three children at a table. They are finishing a box of cookies. A fourth child sees them and runs toward them. The child says:

    (a) Wait! Save me one!

    x (b) Wait! Save one for me!

FOCUS 6 ＞＞＞＞＞＞＞＞＞＞＞＞＞＞＞＞＞＞＞＞＞ FORM

Verbs that Do Not Omit *To* with Indirect Objects

EXAMPLES	EXPLANATIONS
S + V + DO+ IO **(a)** My mother reads stories to us. **S + V + IO + DO** **(b)** My mother reads us stories.	Many verbs follow both Pattern A and B. (See Focus 4.)
DO + IO **(c)** The teacher explains the grammar to us. **(d)** NOT: The teacher explains us the grammar.	Some verbs only follow Pattern A.
explain *describe* *repeat* *introduce* *report* *say* *solve* *open* *carry* *clean* *do* *prepare* *fix* *repair* *spell*	Verbs that follow Pattern A ONLY. Do not omit *to/for*.

Read the following pairs of sentences or questions aloud. Check any sentence that is not possible. In some pairs, both patterns are possible.

EXAMPLE 1:

Pattern A: My husband sends flowers to me every Valentine's Day.

Pattern B: My husband sends me flowers every Valentine's Day.

   (Both patterns are possible.)

EXAMPLE 2:

Pattern A: The teacher always repeats the question to the class.

NOT: **Pattern B:** The teacher always repeats the class the question.

Pattern A

The truth tell to me

1. Tell the truth to me.
2. Please explain the problem to me.
3. Spell that word for me, please.
4. I need to report the accident to the insurance company.
5. My father usually reads a story to my little brother every night.
6. He always opens the door for me.
7. Let me introduce my friend to you.
8. Cynthia gives her old clothes to a charity.
9. The students write letters to their parents every week.
10. Please repeat the instructions to the class.
11. Can you describe your hometown to me?
12. Can you carry that bag for me?

Pattern B

Tell me the truth.

Tell me the truth.

Please explain me the problem.

Spell me that word, please.

I need to report the insurance company the accident.

My father usually reads my little brother a story every night.

He always opens me the door.

Let me introduce you my friend.

Cynthia gives a charity her old clothes.

The students write their parents letters every week.

Please repeat the class the instructions.

Can you describe me your hometown?

Can you carry me that bag?

Activities

ACTIVITY 1

Think of the different things people have. Then give clues so that your classmates can guess the object.

EXAMPLE: Clues: The Japanese make a lot of them. We drive them. What are they?

Answer: Cars!

ACTIVITY 2

STEP 1 Write down the names of ten occupations on ten pieces of paper.

STEP 2 Choose one of the pieces of paper and make sentences for the class so they can guess the profession. You get one point for each sentence you make.

STEP ❸ When the class guesses the profession, another student picks a piece of paper. The person with the most points at the end wins.

EXAMPLE: (You choose "firefighter.")

You say: *This person wears a hat.*

He or she drives a big vehicle.

He or she saves people's lives.

ACTIVITY 3

STEP ❶ Each person in the class writes down a personal habit—good or bad.

STEP ❷ Each person reads his or her statement to the class.

STEP ❸ The class asks questions to find out more information. (Possible habits: playing with your hair, tapping your feet.)

EXAMPLE: You: I *bite my fingernails.*

Class: Why *do you bite them?*

You: *Because I'm nervous!*

ACTIVITY 4

What customs do you have in your country for events such as birth, engagement, marriage, death? Tell the class what people do in your country.

EXAMPLE: In Chile, when a baby is born . . .

when a couple gets married . . .

when someone dies . . .

when a person turns thirteen . . .

OTHER . . .

Work in a small group. On small slips of paper, write the numbers 1 to 16 and put them in an envelope. One person in the class is the "caller" and only he or she looks at the grid below. The first student picks a number from the envelope. The caller calls out the command in that square for the student to follow. Then a second student picks out a number and the caller calls out the command. Continue until all the commands are given.

EXAMPLE: You pick the number 7.

Caller: Lend some money to Maria.

1. Whisper a secret to the person across from you.	2. Give a penny to the person on your left.	3. Write a funny message to someone in your group.	4. Hand your wallet to the person on your right.
5. Make a paper airplane for the person across from you.	6. Tell a funny joke to someone.	7. Lend some money to a person in your group.	8. Describe a friend to someone.
9. Explain indirect objects to the person across from you.	10. Tell your age to the person on your right.	11. Introduce the person on your left to the person on your right.	12. Offer candy to someone.
13. Call up the police and report a crime to them.	14. Open the door for someone in the class.	15. Throw your pen to the person across from you.	16. Pass a secret message to one person in your group.

STEP ❶ Listen to the conversation between Linda and Amy. Then read the statements below. Check True or False.

	True	False
1. Linda is giving her mother perfume on Mother's Day.		
2. Linda's mother tells her what gift she wants.		
3. Amy's mother always tells her daughter what gift she wants.		
4. Linda's father only takes Linda's mother to a restaurant on Mother's Day.		
5. Linda's father does not buy his wife a gift.		

STEP ❷ Work with a partner. If a statement is false, make a true statement.

STEP ❸ Tell your classmates what you do and give to a person on a special day like Mother's Day or a birthday.

UNIT

14

Can, Know How To, Be Able To, And/But/So/Or

Find Someone Who Can . . .

STEP ❶ Find someone in your class who can do these things:

1. dance

2. swim

3. draw

4. sing

5. cook

6. use a computer

7. drive a car

8. play a musical instrument

9. speak three languages

STEP ❷ Report to the class what you know about your classmates.

Can

Can expresses ability.

AFFIRMATIVE	NEGATIVE	NEGATIVE CONTRACTION
I You He She **can** speak We English. You They	I You He She **cannot** We speak Chinese. You They	I You He She **can't** speak We French. You They
(a) She can DANCE. **(b)** He can SING.	In the affirmative, we pronounce *can* as /kən/ and stress the base form of the verb.	
(c) He CAN'T DANCE. **(d)** She CAN'T SING.	In the negative, we stress both *can't* and the base form of the verb.	

EXERCISE I

Go back to the Opening Task on page 205. With a partner, take turns saying what you can or can't do.

EXAMPLE: I can cook.

I can't play a musical instrument.

Make affirmative or negative statements about the pictures.

1. He/hear his mother
   He can't hear his mother.

2. She/swim

3. They/play basketball

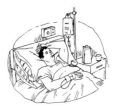

4. She/open the jar

5. He/walk

6. He/go to work

7. They/see the screen

8. They/speak Korean

What can you do in English? Check *Yes* or *No*.

	Yes	No
1. I can introduce someone.		
2. I can ask about prices.		
3. I can describe people and places.		
4. I can make a polite request.		
5. I can give directions.		
6. I can give advice.		
7. I can ask for information about English.		

Now, exchange books with a partner. Tell the class what your partner can or can't do in English.

EXAMPLE: My partner can introduce someone.

FOCUS 2 >>>>>>>>>>>>>>>>>>>>>>>>> FORM

Questions with *Can*

(a) **Can** you use a computer?
Yes, I can. No, I can't.
(b) **Can** he cook?
Yes, he can. No, he can't.

(c) **What** *can* he cook?
He can boil water!
(d) **Who** *can* cook in your family?
My mother can.
My father can't.

EXERCISE 4

STEP ❶ Write *yes/no* questions with *can*. Then, under Your Response, check *Yes* or *No* to give your opinion about each question. Leave the columns under *Total* blank for now.

		Your Response		Total	
		Yes	No	Yes	No
1.	a woman/work as a fire fighter _Can a woman work as a firefighter?_ ?				
2.	women/be good soldiers _____ ?				
3.	a man/be a good nurse _____ ?				
4.	men/raise children _____ ?				

	Your Response		Total	
	Yes	**No**	**Yes**	**No**
5. women/be police officers				
6. a woman/be a construction worker				
7. a man/work as a housekeeper				
8. a woman/be President of a country				
9. a man/work as a baby sitter				

5. women/be police officers

_____ ?

6. a woman/be a construction worker

_____ ?

7. a man/work as a housekeeper

_____ ?

8. a woman/be President of a country

_____ ?

9. a man/work as a baby sitter

_____ ?

STEP ❷ Go back to Exercise 4. Read the questions aloud. Do a survey in your class. Count how many students say "yes" and how many say "no." Write the *total* number of Yes and No answers in the Total column. Do you agree or disagree with your classmates? Give reasons for your answers.

EXAMPLE: Women can be police officers.

They can help people in trouble. They can use guns when necessary.

EXERCISE 5

Work in a group of four to six people. Take turns asking the following questions.

EXAMPLE: a. Who/type?   Who can type?

b. How fast/type?   How fast can you type?

1. a. Who/cook?   b. What/cook?
2. a. Who/speak three languages?   b. What/say in your third language?
3. a. Who/play a musical instrument?   b. What/play?
4. a. Who/sew?   b. What/sew?
5. a. Who/fix a car?   b. What/fix?
6. a. Who/draw?   b. What/draw?
7. a. Who/run a marathon?   b. How fast/run a marathon?

Can, Know How To, Be Able To, And/But/So/Or **209**

Asking for Help with English

EXAMPLES	EXPLANATIONS
(a) Can I say, "She can to swim" **in English?**	When you are not sure your English is correct, use the expression: *Can I say . . . in English?*
(b) How can I say, "..." **in English?**	When you don't know how to say something in English, ask the question: *How can I say, "..." in English?*
	To explain your meaning: Use your hands to show "tremendous."
	Use your face to show "sour."
	Use your whole body to show action like "sweeping."

Look at the pictures. First mime each action and then ask your classmates questions to find out how to say each word.

EXAMPLE: How can I say (mime the action) in English?

1.

2.

3.

4.

5.

6.

FOCUS 4 >>>>>>>>> **FORM/MEANING/USE**

Expressing Ability: *Can, Know How to,* and *Be Able to*

EXAMPLES	EXPLANATIONS
(a) She **can** cook. **(b)** She **knows how to** cook. **(c)** She **is able to** cook.	To express learned ability, use *can, know how to,* or *be able to*.
(d) A blind person **can't** see. **(e)** A blind person **isn't able to** see. **(f)** NOT: A blind person **doesn't know how to** see.	To express natural ability, use *can* or *be able to* only. *Be able to* is more formal than *can*. Use *be able to* in all tenses; not *can*.

Make affirmative or negative statements with the words below. To express learned ability, make one statement with *can* and one statement with *know how to*. To express natural ability, make only one statement with *can*.

EXAMPLES: fix/a flat tire

I can fix a flat tire.

I know how to fix a flat tire.

see/without glasses

I can see without glasses.

1. A blind person/see
2. A dog/live for twenty-five years
3. Infants/walk
4. A deaf person/hear
5. Fish/breathe on land
6. Mechanics/fix cars
7. Men/take care of babies
8. A man/have a baby
9. Doctors/cure some diseases

Fill in the blanks with the affirmative or negative forms of *can* or *be able to*.

Fran: Hello, Vanna. How are you today?

Vanna: I'm sorry to say I'm still not well, Fran. My back still hurts. I (1) _can_ sit up now, but I (2) _am not able to_ walk very well.

Fran: What? You mean you (3) _____ come in to work today? Vanna, I (4) _____ do my work without you. I (5) _____ use my computer. I (6) _____ find any of my papers. I (7) _____

remember any of my appointments. This office is a mess. I (8) _____ do

all this work myself.

Vanna: What about your temporary secretary? What (9) _____ he do?

Fran: This temporary secretary is terrible. He (10) _____ do anything.

He (11) _____ even make a good cup of coffee! I need you here, Vanna.

Only you (12) _____ do everything in this office.

Vanna: Well, Fran, do you remember our conversation about my pay raise?

Fran: O.K., O.K., Vanna. You can have your raise. But please come in today!

Vanna: O.K., calm down, Fran, and listen to me. I (13) _____ come in

to the office this morning, but I (14) _____ come in this afternoon.

Vanna: Oh . . . thank you, Vanna . . . See you later.

EXERCISE 9

Test your knowledge. Make Yes/No Questions and discuss your answers.

1. people/live without food for six months

   Can people live without food for six months?

   Yes, they can.

   No, they can't.

   Are people able to live without food for six months?

   Yes, they are.

   No, they aren't.

2. a computer/think

3. smoking/cause cancer

4. an airplane/fly from New York to Paris in four hours

5. a person/run twenty-five miles an hour

6. a river/flow uphill

7. we/communicate with people from other planets

8. a person/learn a language in one week

9. modern medicine/cure AIDS

10. a two-year old child/read

11. the United Nations/stop wars

12. you/think of any more questions

FOCUS 5 ➤➤➤➤➤➤➤➤➤➤➤➤➤➤ FORM/MEANING

Sentence Connectors:
And/But/So/Or

And, but, so, and **or** are sentence connectors. We use them to connect two complete sentences.

EXAMPLES	EXPLANATIONS
(a) I can rollerskate **and** I can ski.	**And** adds information.
(b) I can dance, **but** I can't sing. He can swim, **but** his brother can't.	**But** shows contrast.
(c) I can't cook, **so** I often go out to eat.	**So** gives a result.
(d) You can go **or** you can stay.	**Or** gives a choice.
(e) I can speak English, but I can't speak Spanish. **(f)** I can speak Spanish, and my sister can speak Japanese.	When you connect two complete sentences, use a comma (,) before the connector.
(g) I can say it in English, or I can say it in French. **(h)** I can say it in English or French.	When the subject is the same for the two verbs, it is not necessary to repeat the subject or *can*. Do not use a comma.

EXERCISE 10

What can you do? Write sentences about yourself with *can* or *know how to* with *and* or *but*.

EXAMPLE: 1. use a typewriter/use a computer

I can use a typewriter, but I can't use a computer.

I can use a typewriter and a computer.

2. rollerskate/rollerblade

3. ride a bicycle/drive a car

4. use a camera/use a video camera

5. use a telephone/use a fax machine

6. cook rice/cook Chinese food

7. sew a button/sew a dress

8. walk fast/run fast

Now make three statements of your own:

9. _____

10. _____

11. _____

EXERCISE 11

Look back at the pictures in Exercise 2. Fill in the blanks with *and*, *but*, or *so*.

1. (Look at Picture 7 in Exercise 2)

Bob and Andrea love the movies, (a) __but__ they are often too busy to go to the movies on Saturdays. They usually go to the first show on Sundays. On Sunday afternoon, the tickets are half-price, (b) _____ the theater is very crowded. There is one woman in the audience who is always a problem. Today, Bob and Andrea are behind her. The woman has very bushy hair, (c) _____ Bob and Andrea can't see the movie screen. She loves pop-corn (d) _____ eats it non-stop during the movie. Popcorn is delicious, (e) _____ it is also very noisy, (f) _____ Bob and Andrea can't hear the movie. Sometimes they think it's better to stay home and rent a movie!

2. (Look at Picture 6 in Exercise 2)

Larry is in the hospital. He has a high fever (a) _____ he is very sick. The doctor wants him to stay in the hospital, (b) _____ Larry wants to go home. The doctor says he needs to rest, (c) _____ Larry wants to go back to work. He is bored in the hospital (d) _____ he misses his family. He is unhappy, (e) _____ he decides to leave.

3. (Look at Picture 1 in Exercise 2)

Tommy loves to listen to loud music, (a) _____ his mom hates his music. Tommy's mom has a headache, (b) _____ she asks Tommy to use his walkman. Tommy has a walkman, (c) _____ it's broken.

Give your partner a choice.

EXAMPLE: listen to rock music / listen to classical music

>**You:** We can listen to rock music or classical music.

>**Your Partner:** Let's listen to rock music.

1. eat at home / go out to a restaurant
2. watch the baseball game on TV / go to the game at the stadium
3. go to an opera / go to a ballet
4. study physics / study biology
5. play cards / watch a movie
6. drive to the mountains / drive to the beach
7, eat Italian food / eat Indian food
8. go to the movies / rent a film and stay home

Activities
ACTIVITY 1

Read the job advertisement in the newspaper for a baby sitter. Interview your partner for the job. Ask questions with *can*, *know how to*, and *be able to*.

EXAMPLE: Do you know how to cook?

>Can you work full-time?

> **WANTED: Baby sitter** Responsible person. Full-time work five days a week 8:00-5:00, some evenings and weekends. Must speak English and be able to drive. Laundry, light housekeeping, and cooking required. Experience with children necessary. References requested.

What can you/do you know how to do that your parents or other people you know cannot/do not know how to do? Write six sentences.

EXAMPLE: My mother can't ride a bicycle, but I can.

My sister knows how to sew, but I don't.

ACTIVITY 3

Do you think it's better to be a man or a woman?
Give as many reasons as you can for your opinion.

EXAMPLE: It's better to be a woman. A woman can have children.

ACTIVITY 4

Make a list of ten jobs.
Say what you can or are able to do. The class decides what job is good for you. Use *and* and *but*.

EXAMPLE: You say: I can help sick people, and get along with them. I am able to follow directions.

Your group: Then you can be a nurse!

ACTIVITY 5

STEP ❶ Ask a classmate if he or she can do one of the activities in the box on the next page.

EXAMPLE: Can you touch your toes?

STEP ❷ If the person says *yes*, write his/her name in the box. Then go to another student and ask another question.
If the person says *no*, ask the other questions until he or she says *yes*. Then write his or her name in the box.

STEP ❸ Each student who answered *yes* must perform the action in the box!

touch your toes	dance	whistle
_____	_____	_____
sing a song in English	say "Hello" in four languages	tell a joke in English
_____	_____	_____
draw a horse	pronounce the word "Psychology"	juggle
_____	_____	_____

ACTIVITY 6

STEP ❶ Listen to Ken's interview for a job. Then answer the questions. Check Yes or No.

	Yes	No
1. Ken can speak French, Spanish, and German.		
2. Ken can stay in another country for a year.		
3. Ken can drive.		
4. Ken can use computers.		
5. Ken can sell computers.		
6. Ken can repair computers.		

STEP ❷ Discuss with your classmates.

1. What kind of job is the interview for?

2. Can Ken get the job? Why or why not?

Present Progressive Tense

A Bad Day at the Harrisons'

Robin's babysitter cannot come today, so her husband Regis is staying at home and taking care of the children and the house.

Talk about what is happening in the picture. Use the subjects on the left and the verbs in the box.

the food

Suzy

the telephone

the baby and the dog

the baby

Jimmy

the dog

Regis

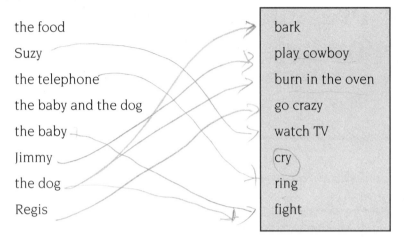

bark

play cowboy

burn in the oven

go crazy

watch TV

cry

ring

fight

Present Progressive: Affirmative Statements

EXAMPLES	EXPLANATIONS
(a) The food **is burning.** **(b)** The baby **is crying.** **(c)** The dog and the baby **are fighting.**	Use the present progressive to talk about an action that is happening right now; an action in progress.
now *right now* *at the moment*	Use these time expressions with the present progressive.

SUBJECT	BE	BASE FORM OF THE VERB + -ING
I	am	
You	are	
He She It	is	working.
We You They	are	

Affirmative Contractions

SUBJECT + BE CONTRACTION	BASE FORM OF THE VERB + -ING
I'm	
You're	
He's She's It's	working.
We're You're They're	

Underline all the present progressive verbs in the text.

EXAMPLE: Regis <u>isn't having</u> a good day.

Today is not a normal day at the Harrisons'. Usually, Robin's babysitter comes at 3:00 when Robin leaves for work. But today, Robin is attending an all-day meeting at the college, and her babysitter can't come. So Regis is spending the day at home. He's taking care of the children and the house. He's trying very hard, but everything is going wrong. Regis isn't having a good day. Actually, poor Regis is going crazy. He's thinking about Robin. He's learning something today. It's not easy to stay home with the children. He's beginning to understand this.

Spelling of Verbs Ending in *-ing*

VERB END	RULE	EXAMPLES	
1. consonant + *e*	Drop the *-e*, add *-ing*.	write	writing
2. vowel + consonant (one syllable)	Double the consonant, add *-ing*.	sit	sitting
Exception: verbs that end in *-w, -x,* and *-y*.	Do not double *w, x,* and *y*.	show fix play	showing fixing playing
3. consonant + vowel + consonant. There is more than one syllable, and the stress is on the last syllable	Double the consonant, add *-ing*.	beGIN forGET	beginning forgetting
If the stress is not on the last syllable	Do not double the consonant.	LISten HAPpen	listening happening
4. *-ie*	Change *-ie* to *y*, add *-ing*.	lie die	lying dying
5. All other verbs	Add *-ing* to the base form of verb.	talk study do agree	talking studying doing agreeing

You can talk with my friend 'Don't forget ?'

EXERCISE 2

Fill in the blanks with the present progressive.

Today's a normal day at the Harrisons'. It is 4:00. Robin (1) __Preparing__ (prepare) dinner in the kitchen. She (2) __Slicing__ (slice) onions and (3) __wiping__ (wipe) the tears from her eyes. The house is quiet, so she (4) __listening__ (listen) to some music. She (5) __thinking__ (think) about her class tonight. She (6) __waiting__ (wait) for her babysitter to arrive.

The baby (7) _____Sleeping_____ (sleep). The dog (8) _____Chewing_____ (chew) on a bone. Jimmy (9) _____Playing_____ (play) with his toys. Suzy (10) _____Cleaning_____ (clean) her room. Everything is under control.

EXERCISE 3

Who's talking? Fill in the blanks with the present progressive of the verb. Then match each statement to a picture.

EXAMPLE: "You're ___driving___ (drive) me crazy. Turn off the TV!"

c 1. "That crazy dog _____biting_____ (bite) me!"

a.

d 2. "I _I'm walking_ (walk) into a zoo!"

b.

e 3. "Quiet! You _are making_ (make) a lot of noise. I can't hear the TV."

c.

b 4 "Stop that, Jimmy. You _are hurting_ (hurt) me."

d.

a 5. "Oh no! The food _is burning_ (burn)!"

e.

f 6. "I _'m dying_ (die) to take off my shoes. My feet _are killing_ (kill) me."

f.

Present Progressive: Negative Statements

SUBJECT + BE + NOT			NEGATIVE CONTRACTION			BE CONTRACTION + NOT		
I	am		*			I'm		
You	are		You	aren't		You're		
He She It	is	not working.	He She It	isn't	working.	He's She's It's		not working.
We You They	are		We You They	aren't		We're You're They're		

*There is no standard English contraction with I *am not.*

Make sentences with negative contractions.

EXAMPLE: Robin/take care of the children today

Robin isn't taking care of the children today.

1. Robin/wear comfortable shoes today
2. Robin's babysitter/come today
3. The baby and the dog/get along
4. Regis/relax
5. The children/listen to Regis
6. Suzy/do her homework
7. Suzy/help Regis
8. Regis/pay attention to the dinner in the oven
9. Regis/laugh
10. Regis/enjoy his children today

Look at the picture. Make affirmative or negative statements.

EXAMPLE: Mrs. Bainbridge _is having_ (have) a party at her home this evening.

Mrs Bainbridge _isn't talking_ (talk) to her guests at the moment.

Mrs. Bainbridge is having a party at her home this evening. The guests
(1) ___are___ (talk) in the living room. But Mr. and Mrs. Parker
(2) ___aren't___ (talk) to the other guests. They (3) ___are enjoying___
(enjoy) the party. They (4) ___aren't feeling___ (feel) very bored right now. They
(5) ___aren't thinking of___ (think of) a way to escape. Mrs. Bainbridge
(6) ___isn't standing___ (stand) in the doorway. She (7) ___isn't turning___
(turn) her back to the Parkers. The Parkers (8) ___aren't leaving___ (leave),
but they (9) ___aren't leaving___ by the front door. Mr. and Mrs. Parker
(10) ___are___ (climb) out of the bedroom window at the moment.

226   *Unit 15*

Mr. Parker (11) _is holding_ (hold) his hat between his teeth.

He (12) _is helping_ (help) Mrs. Parker climb out. Mr. and

Mrs. Parker (13) _aren't saying_ (say) good-bye to the other guests.

 FOCUS 4 >>>>>>>>>>>>>>>>>>>>>>>>>>> USE

Choosing Simple Present or Present Progressive

The simple present and the present progressive have different uses.

USE THE SIMPLE PRESENT FOR:	USE THE PRESENT PROGRESSIVE FOR:
• **habits and repeated actions**	• **actions in progress now**
(a) Suzy usually does her homework in the afternoon.	**(b)** Suzy's watching TV right now.
• **things that are true in general**	• **actions that are temporary, not habitual**
(c) Women usually take care of children.	**(d)** Regis is taking care of the children today.
	• **situations that are changing**
	(e) These days, men are spending more time with their children.

Time Expressions		Time Expressions	
always	_rarely_	_right now_	_now_
often	_never_	_today_	_at the moment_
usually	_every day_	_this week_	_this evening_
sometimes	_once a week_	_this year_	_this month_
seldom	_on the weekends_	_these days_	

EXERCISE 6

Read each statement. If the statement is in the simple present, make a second statement in the present progressive. If the statement is in the present progressive, make a second statement in the simple present.

Simple Present	Present Progressive
1. Suzy usually does her homework in the evening.	a. _Tonight she is watching cartoons on TV._
2. _____	b. Tonight, Robin isn't cooking dinner.
3. Robin usually takes care of the children.	c. _____
4. _____	d. Today, Regis is spending the day at home.
5. The baby sitter usually takes care of the children when Robin goes to work.	e. _____
6. _____	f. Right now, the baby and the dog are fighting.
7. The babysitter usually doesn't go crazy.	g. _____

EXERCISE 7

Make sentences with *these days* or *today* to show changing situations.

EXAMPLE: women/get more education

These days, women are getting more education.

1. Women/get good jobs
2. Fifty percent of American women/ work outside the home
3. Women/earn money
4. Women/become more independent

5. Men/share the work in the home
6. Husbands/help their wives
7. Fathers/spend more time with their children
8. The roles of men and women/change

Add two sentences of your own.

9. _____

10. _____

Verbs Not Usually Used in the Progressive

There are some verbs we usually do not use in the present progressive. These verbs are *not* action verbs. They are called nonprogressive (or stative) verbs.

EXAMPLES	NONPROGRESSIVE (STATIVE) VERBS
(a) Robin **loves** her job. **(b)** NOT: Robin is loving her job. **(c)** The children **need** help. **(d)** NOT: The children are needing help.	**FEELINGS AND EMOTIONS** (*like, love, hate, prefer, want, need*)
(e) Regis **understands** his wife.	**MENTAL STATES** (*think, believe, understand, seem, forget, remember, know, mean*)
(f) Regis **hears** the telephone ringing.	**SENSES** (*hear, see, smell, taste, feel, sound*)
(g) Robin and Regis **own** a house.	**POSSESSION** (*belong, own, have*)

There are some stative verbs you can use in the present progressive, but they have a different meaning.

SIMPLE PRESENT	PRESENT PROGRESSIVE
(h) I **think** you're a good student. (*Think* means "believe.")	**(i)** I **am thinking** about you now.
(j) I **have** two cars. (*Have* means "possess.")	**(k)** I'm **having** a good time. (*Have* describes the experience.)
(l) This soup **tastes** delicious. (*Taste* means "how the food is.")	**(m)** I'm **tasting** the soup. (*Taste* here means the person is putting soup in his or her mouth.)

EXERCISE 8

Fill in the blanks with the present progressive or simple present form of the verb. Read the dialogues aloud. Use contractions.

EXAMPLE: Regis: _I'm going_ (go) crazy in this house.

   Robin: _I think_ (think) you need a vacation!

1. **Regis:** Suzy, I need your help here.

   Suzy: But, Dad, you (a) ___need___ (need) my help every five minutes! I (b) _am watching_ (watch) TV right now!

2. It is 3:00. The telephone rings.

   Regis: Hello.

   Laura: Hello, Regis. What are you (a) ___doing___ (do) home in the middle of the afternoon?

   Regis: Oh, hi, Laura. I know I (b) ___am___ (be) never home in the afternoon, but today I (c) ___am trying___ (try) to be a househusband!

   Laura: Oh really? Where's Robin?

   Regis: Robin (d) ___is attending___ (attend) a meeting at the college, so I (e) _I am take care of_ (take care of) the kids.

3. Jimmy interrupts Regis's telephone conversation:

   Regis: Hold on a minute, Laura . . . Jimmy (a) _is pulling_ (pull) on my leg! Jimmy, I (b) _am talking_ (talk) to Mommy's friend Laura right now. You (c) ___know___ (know) Laura. She (d) _is coming_ (come) to see Mommy every week. Now, just wait a minute, please . . .

   Laura: Is everything O.K., Regis?

   Regis: Oh, yes, Laura, don't worry. We (e) _are doing_ (do) just fine. Talk to you later; bye!

4. It is 5:30. The telephone rings.

   Regis: Hello.

   Robin: Hi, honey! The meeting (a) ___is___ (be) over. I (b) ___am___ (be) on my way home. What (c) _is happening_ (happen)? I hope the children (d) _are behaving_ (behave).

Regis: They (e) _are acting_ (act) like wild animals, Robin. I (f) _am yelling_ (yell) at them all the time, but they don't listen to me. I (g) _am not having_ (not/have) a very good day today. Please come home soon.

Robin: You (h) _____ sound _____ (sound) terrible! Can I bring anything home, dear?

Regis: Yes, a bottle of aspirin!

EXERCISE 9

Work with a partner. You describe a picture by making one statement with *seem*, *look*, or *feel* and an adjective from the box and another statement with the present progressive to say what the person is doing. Your partner tells you the number of the picture you are talking about. Take turns.

EXAMPLE: You say: The boy looks sad. He is crying.

    Your partner says: Picture Number 1.

sad ✔	sick	scared	tired
angry	happy	cold	hot
bored	surprised	nervous	confused

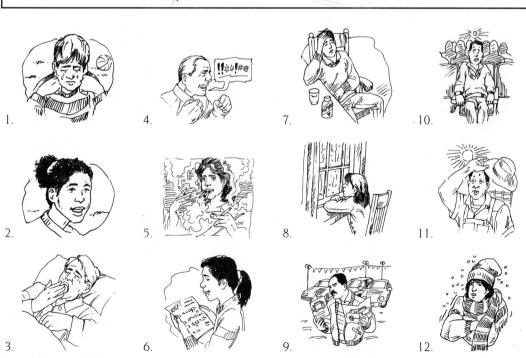

1.   4.   7.   10.

2.   5.   8.   11.

3.   6.   9.   12.

FOCUS 6 >>>>>>>>>>>>>>>>>>>>>>>>> **FORM**

Present Progressive: Yes/No Questions and Short Answers

YES/NO QUESTIONS			SHORT ANSWERS					
Am	I		Yes,	you	are.	No,	you	aren't.
Are	you		Yes,	I	am.	No,	I'm	not.
Is	he he it	working?	Yes,	he she it	is.	No,	he she it	isn't.
Are	you we they		Yes,	we you they	are.	No,	we you they	aren't.

EXERCISE 10

With a partner, take turns asking and answering questions about the Harrisons. Give short answers. Use the verbs from the box below.

EXAMPLE: Suzy/ . . . /her father

Is Suzy helping her father? No, she isn't.

watch	ring	play	bite	come
burn		help	fight	smile

1. children / their father
2. Frankie and the dog/ . . .
3. Suzy / TV
4. their dinner/ . . .
5. the phone/ . . .

6. Jimmy / cowboy
7. the dog / the toy
8. Robin / home
9. Robin

Work with a partner and ask each other Yes/No questions about your life these days. Check Yes or No.

EXAMPLE: enjoy English class

Are you enjoying your English class?

your English/improve

Is your English improving?

You		Your Partner	
Yes	No	Yes	No

1. enjoy English class?
2. your English/improve?
3. take other classes?
4. learn a lot?
5. get good grades?
6. make progress?
7. do a lot of homework?
8. cook for yourself?
9. go out with friends?
10. meet lots of people?
11. eat well?
12. sleep well?
13. get exercise?
14. work after school?

Present Progressive: *Wh*-Questions

WH-WORD	BE	SUBJECT	VERB + -ING	ANSWERS
What	am	I	doing?	(You're) getting ready for the beach.
When **Where** **Why** **How**	are	you	going?	(I'm going) at 2:00. (We're going) to the beach. (We're going) because we don't have school today. (We're going) by car.
Who(m)	is	she	meeting?	(She's meeting) her friends.
Who*	is		having a nice day?	Clara (is having a nice day).

*Who is asking about the subject.

EXERCISE 12

Write the question that asks for the underlined information.

1. **Q:** Who is watching television?

   A: <u>Suzy</u> is watching television.

2. **Q:** Who(m) is Regis taking care of tonight?

   A: Regis is taking care of <u>the children</u>.

3. **Q:** _____

   A: Frankie and the dog are fighting <u>because they both want the toy.</u>

4. **Q:** _____

   A: Robin is meeting <u>her colleagues</u> at the college.

5. **Q:** _____

   A: Robin's thinking that <u>she's lucky to be at work!</u>

6. **Q:** _____

   A: They're eating sandwiches for dinner <u>because Regis's dinner tastes terrible.</u>

7. **Q:** _____

   A: <u>Regis</u> is watching the children today.

8. **Q:** _____

   A: Regis is taking two aspirin <u>because he has a terrible headache.</u>

9. **Q:** _____

   A: Robin's meeting is taking place <u>at the college.</u>

10. **Q:** _____

    A: <u>Robin</u> is coming home right now.

11. **Q:** _____

    A: Regis is feeling <u>very tired</u> right now.

12. **Q:** _____

    A: <u>The children</u> are making a lot of noise.

EXERCISE 13

Correct the mistakes in the following sentences.

EXAMPLE: Is the pizza tasting good?

Does the pizza taste good?

1. Frankie and the dog are fight. *Frankie and the dog are fighting?*
2. He's having a new TV. *He has a new TV.*
3. Why you are working today? *Who are you doing today?*
4. Are you needing my help? *Do you need my help?*
5. What Robin is thinking? *What is Robin thinking.*
6. Is she believing him? *Does she believe him?*
7. Right now, he plays cowboy on his father's back. *Right now, he is playing cowboy on his father's back.*
8. The soup is smelling bad. *The soup smells bad.*
9. Where you are going? *Where are you going?*
10. People no are saving money nowadays. *People aren't saving money nowadays.*
11. You working hard these days. *You are working hard these days.*
12. How you doing today? *What are you doing today?*

Activities

ACTIVITY 1

Your teacher will divide the class into two groups.

STEP ① Group A should look at the statements in Column A. One student at a time will mime an action. Students in Group B must guess the action. Group B students can ask questions of Group A. Then Group B mimes statements from Column B and Group A guesses the action.

Column A	Column B
1. You are opening the lid of a jar. The lid is on very tight.	2. You are reading a very sad story.
3. You are watching a very funny TV show.	4. You are an expectant father waiting in the delivery room.
5. You are trying to sleep and a mosquito is bothering you.	6. You are sitting at the bar in a noisy disco. At the other side of the bar, there is someone you like. You are trying to get that person's attention.
7. You are crossing a busy street. You are holding a young child by the hand and carrying a bag of groceries in the other hand.	8. You are a dinner guest at a friend's house. Your friend is not a good cook. You don't like the food!
9. You are trying to thread a needle, but you're having trouble finding the eye of the needle.	10. You are cutting up onions to cook dinner.

STEP ② Make up three situations like those above. Write each situation on a separate piece of paper and put all the situations in a hat. Every student will then pick a situation and mime it for the others to guess.

ACTIVITY 2

In this unit, we see that family life is changing in the United States. Is family life changing in the country you come from or in a country that you know? Write sentences using the simple present and present progressive tense about the following.

Mothers . . .   Grandparents . . .
Fathers . . .   Couples . . .
Children . . .   Men . . .
Teenagers . . .   Women . . .

LISTEN AND DECIDE

STEP ❶ Look at the three pictures. Listen to the conversation. Decide which picture fits the description. Check A, B, or C.

A.

B.

C.

The woman is describing Picture   A ——————   B ——————   C ——————

STEP ❷ Describe the other two girls in the picture.

STEP ❶ Look at the picture. Give this person a name, nationality, occupation, age, and so on. Write a story about this person. What is the woman doing? Where is she? How does she look? What is she thinking about? Why is she there?

STEP ❷ Tell the class your story.

Adjective Phrases

Another, The Other, Other(s),
The Other(s), Intensifiers

OPENING TASK

Meeting the Staff at P.S. 31

Identify the people below by describing them. Do not point to the pictures. Say what each person does at P.S. 31.

A.

B.

C.

D.

E.

F.

1. ——— is the school principal.

2. ——— teaches science.

3. ——— is the school nurse.

4. ——— is the girls' basketball coach.

5. ——— works in the school cafeteria.

6. ——— teaches art.

Adjective Phrases

EXAMPLES			EXPLANATIONS
Noun	Adjective Phrase	Verb	
(a) The man	**in the suit**	is the school principal.	Adjective phrases are groups of words that describe nouns.
(b) The food	**on the table**	is delicious.	
The woman is in a white coat. The woman is the school nurse.			Adjective phrases can combine two sentences.
(c) The woman	**in a white coat**	is the school nurse.	
(d) The **man** with the books **is** the science teacher.			The verb agrees with the subject, not with the noun in the adjective phrase.

EXERCISE 1

Put parentheses around the adjective phrases. Underline the subject and the verb in each sentence.

EXAMPLE: The man (in the suit) works in an office.

1. The man in the suit and tie is the school principal.

2. The man with the books and microscope is the science teacher.

3. The woman in the white coat is the school nurse.

4. The woman with the whistle is the girls' basketball coach.

5. The man with the white hat works in the school cafeteria.

6. The woman with the easel and paints is the art teacher.

Each chair belongs to one of the people on the next page. Match each person to a chair. Then write a sentence with an adjective phrase.

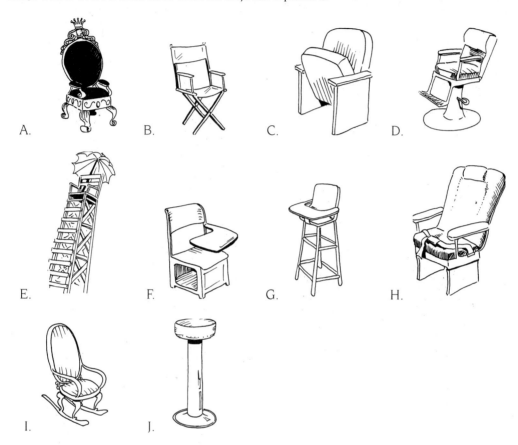

A.

B.

C.

D.

E.

F.

G.

H.

I.

J.

1. 2. 3. 4.

5. 6. 7. 8.

9. 10.

Chair	Person	
1. A	7	The man with the crown sits in chair A.
2.		
3.		
4.		
5.		
6.		
7.		
8.		
9.		
10.		

Combine each of the sentence pairs into one sentence with an adjective phrase. Then identify the person in the picture and write the number of your sentence next to the person.

1. The girl has pigtails. She is kicking her partner.

   The girl with pigtails is kicking her partner.

2. The boy has a striped shirt and black pants. He is throwing a paper airplane across the room.

   _____

3. The girls are near the window. They are waving to their friends outside.

   _____

4. The boy is in a baseball uniform. He is standing on the teacher's desk.

   _____

5. The boys are in the back of the room. They are fighting.

   _____

6. The boy is in the corner. He is reading.

   _____

7. The girl is in the closet. She is crying.

   _____

8. The girl has a Walkman. She is singing.

   _____

9. The man has a rope around him. He is the new teacher.

   _____

10. The man is in a suit and tie. He is the school principal.

   _____

Questions with *Which*

EXAMPLES	EXPLANATIONS
(a) **Which** woman is wearing a white coat? the school nurse (b) **Which** teachers are women? the coach and the art teacher	Use *which* when there is a choice between two or more people or things.
(c) **Which** coat do you like, Mom? I like the black **one.** (d) **Which** shoes do you like, Dad? the brown **ones**	Substitute the words *one* or *ones* for nouns so you do not repeat the noun.
(e) **Which** shoes do you want? the ones **in the window**	You can also use adjective phrases after *one* and *ones*.

Julie's house was robbed. She is talking to her husband on the phone, describing the damage. Work with a partner. Find the differences between the pictures. You say Julie's statements. Your partner is the husband, and asks questions with *which* to get more specific information.

EXAMPLE: **Julie:** The window is broken.

Husband: Which window?

Julie: The one over the kitchen sink.

BEFORE

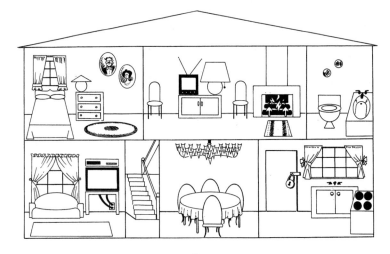

AFTER

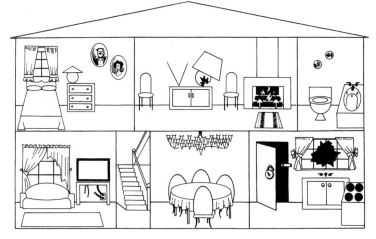

1. The window is broken.
2. The curtains are torn.
3. The TV is missing.

4. The door is open.
5. The lamp is broken.
6. The VCR over the TV is missing.

7. The lock is broken.
8. The rug is missing.

Another, The Other, Other(s), The Other(s)

	ADJECTIVE	PRONOUN	MEANING
A: I'm hungry. B: Here. Have a cookie. A: I am still hungry. Can I have **another** cookie? (Can I have **another**?)	**another** cookie	**another**	one more cookie; one more from a group
B: There are no more cookies in the box. A: There are two **other boxes** in the closet. (There are two **others** in the closet.)	**other** boxes	**others**	more than one more
B: I found one box. Where is **the other box**? (Where is **the other**?) B: **The other box** is behind it. A: How many more cookies can I have?	**the other** box	**the other**	the one you spoke about; the last one in a group
B: You can have one more. **The other cookies** are for me! (**The others** are for me!)	**the other** cookies	**the others**	the ones you spoke about; the last ones in a group

EXERCISE 5

Thor is visiting Earth from another planet. Ed Toppil interviews Thor on television.

Fill in the blanks with *another, the other, other(s),* or *the other(s)*.

Ed: We on Earth are really excited to know there is (1) _____ planet

out there, Thor. Many of us know there are (2) _____ , but we are not able

to find them. Do you know of any (3) _____ planets?

Thor: Yes, we do. We know two (4) _____: Limbix and Cardiax. I have photos of the people from both of (5) _____ planets.

The Limbix are the ones on the left. The Cardiax are (6) _____ ones. We also now know the planet Earth. We are sure there are (7) _____ out there, but (8) _____ are very far away.

Ed: I am surprised that you speak English so well, Thor. Do the Thoraxes have (9) _____ language too?

Thor: Yes, of course. We speak Thoracic, but English is a universal language, you know, so we all learn it in school. People on (10) _____ two planets speak English too!

Ed: So what brings you to Earth?

Thor: Well, Ed, we are looking for (11) _____ intelligent beings in the universe.

Ed: On Earth?!! I don't know if you can find many intelligent beings on Earth, Thor! But we can discuss this at (12) _____ time. Right now, let's stop for a station break.

EXERCISE 6

Thor tours America. Fill in *another*, *other*(s), or *the other*(s).

1. **George:** You only have one tie, Thor. You need to buy (a) _____ one.

Thor: Why?

George: Because Americans are consumers. They like to buy things.

Thor: But I don't like any (b) _____ ties here.

George: O.K. Look at (c) _____ over there. Maybe you can find (d) _____ one.

2. Thor is in a candy store with a child:

    Thor: Which candy is good here?

    Child: This one is good, but first taste (a) _____ one in the brown and green paper. It's out of this world!

    Thor: Hmmmm, excellent. Is it O.K. to take (b) _____ one?

3. **Soaprah:** So, Thor, tell us about your family. Are you married?

Thor: Yes. I am, and I have two children. One is a specialist in interplanetary communication and (a) _____ owns a spaceship factory.

Soaprah: And what does your wife do?

Thor: My wife is a spaceship pilot.

Soaprah: What about (b) _____ people on Thorax? What do they do?

Thor: (c) _____ do different jobs. We have doctors, teachers, artists, and so on. We don't have any tax collectors.

Soaprah: Are there any (d) _____ professions you don't have?

Thor: We don't have any lawyers, I'm happy to say.

Soaprah: That sounds great to me!

Thor: Do you have any (e) _____ questions?

Soaprah: I have a million (f) _____ questions! But our time is up. It was nice meeting you, Thor. Thanks so much for coming.

Intensifiers

Intensifiers are words that make adjectives more or less strong.

SUBJECT	BE	INTENSIFIER	ADJECTIVE
(a) Earth	is	very	beautiful.
(b) The people on Thorax	are	quite	similar.
(c) The people on Earth	are	rather/pretty* fairly	different.
(d) Thorax	isn't	very**	beautiful.

SUBJECT	BE	ARTICLE	INTENSIFIER	ADJECTIVE	NOUN
(e) Earth	is	a	very	special	place.
(f) Thorax	is	a	rather/pretty fairly	small	planet.
(g) Thorax	isn't	a	very	attractive	place.

Pretty has the same meaning as *rather*, but is very informal.
**Very* is the only intensifier we use in negative sentences.

SUBJECT	BE	INTENSIFIER	ARTICLE	ADJECTIVE	NOUN
(h) Thorax	is	quite	a	small	planet.

Test Thor's knowledge. How many of the objects can Thor (and you) guess?

1. This is fairly long and thin.

   People eat it.

   It is very popular in Italy.

   What is it? _____

2. This is a liquid.

   People usually drink it hot.

   They like its rather strong smell.

   It is brown.

   What is it? _____

3. This is an electrical appliance.

   It is quite common in people's homes.

   Sometimes it is very hot.

   You put bread into it.

   What is it? _____

4. This is very cold.

   It's also pretty hard.

   People put it in drinks on hot days.

   It's quite slippery.

   What is it? _____

5. This is quite a big metal box.

   It's electrical and pretty practical.

   It's very useful in tall buildings.

   People go inside the box.

   The box goes up and down.

   What is it? _____

6. This is a very popular piece of plastic.

   It isn't very big.

   With it, we can buy rather expensive things without money.

   What is it? _____

7. There are different kinds of candy.

   All of them are good.

   But this one is very special.

   It comes in brown or white.

   It's pretty fattening.

   It's quite delicious.

   What is it? _____

8. This thing is quite colorful.

   It isn't very common.

   It sometimes follows rainstorms.

   It is quite a beautiful sight.

   What is it? _____

EXERCISE 8

Ed Toppil continues his interview with Thor. Write an intensifier in each blank. There is more than one possible answer.

Ed: So tell me, Thor, what do you think of our planet?

Thor: Well, Earth is a beautiful planet, but it's (1) __quite_____ a strange place. Many of your leaders are not doing a (2) _____ good job. Some people on Earth are (3) _____ rich. Others are (4) _____ poor. There can be a (5) _____ big difference among people. On Thorax, we are all equal. Money isn't (6) _____ important. Learning is

(7) _____ important. That's why we're visiting Earth. Your knowledge can

be (8) _____ useful to us. Also, your art and music are

(9) _____ beautiful.

Ed: That's (10) _____ interesting. I'm sure we can learn many

(11) _____ useful and exciting things from you, too, Thor.

EXERCISE 9

How necessary or important is each thing? Make statements about Thor's opinion, and give your opinion. Use intensifiers. Explain your answers.

1. a spaceship

   For me, a spaceship is not necessary. I travel by car.

   For Thor, a spaceship is very important. Thor travels by spaceship.

2. a car	8. a good leader for the country
3. a spaceship	9. a computer
4. a credit card	10. teachers
5. music	11. a beautiful planet
6. knowledge	12. friends
7. money	

EXERCISE 10

Fill in a verb (affirmative or negative) and an intensifier in each blank. There are many possible answers. Talk about your answers with a partner.

1. A walkman _is fairly_____ useful.

2. A cordless telephone _____ practical.

3. Big cars _____ economical.

4. A microwave oven _____ necessary.

5. A driver's license _____ important.

6. A credit card _____ dangerous.

7. Fast food _____ popular in my country.

8. American movies _____ violent.

9. Airplanes _____ safe.

10. A university degree _____ important.

Activities

ACTIVITY 1

STEP ❶ Write ten sentences that give information about your country or city. Use adjective phrases.

EXAMPLE: The beaches in the south are beautiful.

The market in the center of the city is always crowded.

The coffee in Brazil is delicious.

STEP ❷ Now tell the class about your country or city.

ACTIVITY 2

STEP ❶ In a group, write sentences about ten students in the class. Use adjective phrases. Do not use names.

STEP ❷ Read your sentences to the class. The class guesses the person you are talking about.

EXAMPLE: The student from Bogota has pretty eyes.

The student next to Miyuki wears glasses.

The student with the big smile is from Ecuador.

ACTIVITY 3

STEP ❶ Check (✔)the adjectives that describe you, and write *very/quite/rather/pretty/fairly/not very* under You in the chart on the next page.

STEP ❷ Ask your partner questions to find out which adjectives describe him or her. Then ask questions with *how* and write *very/quite/rather/pretty/fairly/not very* under Your Partner in the same chart.

EXAMPLE: You ask: Are you shy?

Your partner answers: Yes, I am.

You ask: How shy are you?

Your partner answers: I'm very shy.

	You		Your Partner	
Adjective		very quite rather pretty fairly not very		very quite rather pretty fairly not very
shy				*very*
lazy				
quiet				
romantic				
friendly				
old-fashioned				
organized				
jealous				
talkative				
athletic				
healthy				

ACTIVITY 4

Use the information in Activity 3 to write five sentences about you or about your partner using *very/quite/rather/pretty/fairly/not very*.

EXAMPLE: My partner is a very romantic person. He is pretty old-fashioned, and he is very jealous.

Imagine you are starting life on a new planet. Look at the list of people. Then choose only ten people to move to the new planet. Say how necessary each one is and why.

EXAMPLE: A doctor is very necessary because we need to stay healthy.

an actor	an artist	a police officer	a political leader
a scientist	a religious leader	a young man	a young woman
a historian	a writer	musician	a lawyer
a farmer	a teacher	a journalist	a pilot
a doctor	a mechanic	a computer specialist	a dancer
a military person		an elderly person	an engineer

ACTIVITY 6

Make up descriptions of objects using intensifiers like those in Exercise 7. Test your classmates' knowledge of these objects.

ACTIVITY 7

STEP ❶ Listen to the three descriptions and say who is Bob, Don, and Tom.

STEP ❷ Work in a group. Each student draws a face. Then, the student describes the face to the rest of the group. The rest of the group draws what the student describes.

UNIT
17
Past Tense of B*e*

OPENING TASK

Test Your Memory

Look at the photos and the information about famous people from the past. Make statements about each person. Correct any facts that are not true. See answers on page AK-1.

		Nationality	Occupation
	1. Martin Luther King, Jr.	African	civil rights leader
	2. The Beatles	British	hairdressers
	3. Marilyn Monroe	American	actress

4. Indira Gandhi

Indian

rock singer

5. Pierre and Marie Curie

French

fashion designers

6. Mao

Chinese

political leader

7. Jacqueline Kennedy Onassis

Greek

millionaire

8. George Washington,
Thomas Jefferson,
Abraham Lincoln,
Theodore Roosevelt

Canadian

presidents

FOCUS 1 >>>>>>>>>>>>>>>>>>>>>>>> **FORM**

Past Tense of Be:
Affirmative Statements

SUBJECT	VERB	
I	was	
You	were	
He She It	was	famous.
We You They	were	
There There	was were	a famous actress in that film. many political leaders at the meeting.

EXERCISE 1

Use the past tense of *be* to make correct statements about the famous people in the Opening Task.

1. The Beatles _____Was_____ a famous British rock group in the 1960s.

2. Indira Gandhi _____Was_____ the Prime Ministers of India.

3. Marie and Pierre Curie _____were_____ French scientists.

4. Mao Tse Toung _____was_____ a revolutionary and political leader in the People's Republic of China.

5. George Washington, Thomas Jefferson, Abraham Lincoln, and Theodore Roosevelt _____were_____ presidents of the United States.

6. Martin Luther King, Jr., _____Was_____ an American civil rights leader.

7. Marilyn Monroe _____was_____ an American movie star.

8. Jacqueline Kennedy Onassis _____was_____ the wife of president John F. Kennedy and of Aristotle Onassis, a Greek millionaire.

Fill in the blanks in the postcard. Use *be* in the simple past.

Dear Grandma and Grandpa,

Here we are in Florida. What a place! Yesterday

we (1) __were__ at Disneyworld all day. The sun

(2) __was__ really strong and it (3) __was__ very hot.

The lines (4) __was__ long, but the rides and the shows

(5) __were__ fun. Disneyworld (6) __was__ crowded,

but all the people (7) __were__ friendly and polite. Our

favorite place (8) __were__ Cinderella's palace! The

fireworks at night (9) __was__ beautiful! It

(10) __was__ great for us, but Dad (11) __was__

really hot and tired at the end of the day!

We miss you! See you soon.

Love, Melanie and Michele

The Grandparents
Homestead Lane
Harvard, MA
01451

Orlando FL
FL
34624

USA
20

Past Tense of B*e*:
Negative Statements

SUBJECT	BE + NOT			NEGATIVE CONTRACTIONS	
I	was not		I	wasn't	
You	were not		You	weren't	
He She It	was not	famous.	He She It	wasn't	famous.
We You They	were not		We You They	weren't	
There	was	no time to eat.	There	wasn't	any time to eat.
There	were	no dates in the Task.	There	weren't	any dates in the Task.

EXERCISE 3

How do Michael and Carol remember their trip to Disneyworld? Fill in the blanks with the affirmative or negative of *be* in the simple past. Then role-play the dialogue aloud.

Alice: Oh, hi, Michael. Hi, Carol. How (1) __was__ your trip to Disneyworld last week?

Carol: Hi, Alice. Oh, it (2) __was__ fun.

Michael: Fun! That vacation (3) __wasn't__ (not) fun, it (4) __was__ terrible!

Carol: But Michael, how can you say that? I think the children and I (5) __were__ very satisfied with our vacation.

Michael: Carol, the weather (6) __was__ boiling hot.

Carol: It (7) __wasn't__ (not) boiling hot, it (8) __was__ very comfortable.

Michael: The food (9) ___wasn't___ (not) very good . . .

Carol: The food (10) ___was.___ fine, Michael.

Michael: The people (11) ___were___ (not) friendly.

Carol: Of course, they (12) ___were___ friendly.

Michael: The kids (13) ___were___ very difficult.

Carol: The kids (14) ___weren't___ (not) difficult, Michael. Come on, they (15) ___were___ great.

EXERCISE 4

Make sentences about last weekend with the adjectives in the box.

cheap	cold	rainy	polite	sunny	rude	good
interesting	friendly	windy	comfortable	terrible	slow	charming
warm	small	wet	nice	delicious	crowded	wonderful

Last weekend, you were in the country with your friends . . .

1. The weather? How was the weather?

   It was cold. _____

2. In the evening, you were at an expensive restaurant.

   How was the restaurant? The food and service?

   _____

3. After the restaurant, you were at a party.

   How were the people?

   _____

EXERCISE 5

Do you remember the story Cinderella. Fill in the blanks with the affirmative or negative form of *be*.

Once upon a time, there (1) _____ a young woman named Cinderella.
She (2) _____ rich, but she (3) _____ very beautiful and kind.
Her two stepsisters (4) _____ beautiful. They (5) _____ jealous
of Cinderella. Cinderella's stepmother (6) _____ good to her.

Yes/No Questions and Short Answers with *Be* in the Simple Past

YES/NO QUESTIONS			SHORT ANSWERS		
VERB	SUBJECT		AFFIRMATIVE		NEGATIVE
Was	I			you were.	you were not. / you weren't.
Were	you			I was.	I was not. / I wasn't.
Was	he she it	right?	Yes,	he she was. it	No, he/she/it was not. / he/she/it wasn't.
Were	we you they			you we were. they	you/we/ were not. they / you/we/ weren't. they
Was there any good food at Disneyworld?			Yes,	there was.	No, there was not. / No, there wasn't.
Were there long lines at Disneyworld?			Yes,	there were	No, there were not. / No, there weren't.

EXERCISE 6

Detective Furlock Humes is questioning a police officer about a crime. Fill in the blanks with *there + be* in the simple past.

EXAMPLE: ___Was there___ a crime last night?

___There were___ several police officers at the house.

Police Officer: The body was here, Detective Humes.

Furlock: (1) _____ a weapon?

Police Officer: Yes, (2) _____ a gun next to the body.

Furlock: (3) _____ any fingerprints on the gun?

Police Officer: No, sir, (4) _____ .

Furlock: (5) _____ any motive for this crime?

Police Officer: We don't know, sir.

Furlock: How about witnesses? (6) _____ any witnesses to the crime?

Police Officer: Yes, sir. (7) _____ one witness—a neighbor. She said (8) _____ loud noises in the apartment at midnight.

Furlock: Where is she? Bring her to me . . .

EXERCISE 7

Ask your classmates Yes/No questions about the events below. Give short answers. Correct the facts if necessary.

EXAMPLE: Margaret Thatcher/the first female Prime Minister of Great Britain.

Was Margaret Thatcher the first female Prime Minister of Great Britain?

Yes, she was.

1. Tom Hanks/the first man to walk on the moon
2. AIDS/a known disease in 1949
3. Yugoslavia/a country in 1980
4. Europeans/the first people on the American continent
5. Nelson Mandela/in prison for many years in South Africa
6. The Wright Brothers/the first men to cross the Atlantic Ocean by plane
7. a big earthquake/in Kobe, Japan in 1995
8. any women/in the Olympic Games in 1920

Wh-Questions with Be

WH-QUESTION	BE	SUBJECT	ANSWERS
What		November 22, 1963?	It was the day of President Kennedy's assassination.
Where		the assassination?	It was in Dallas, Texas.
How	was	the day?	Very sad.
Who		the assassin?	Lee Harvey Oswald, we think.
When		the assassination?	November 22, 1963.
Why	were	people sad?	because Kennedy was a popular president.
Whose gun	was	it?	Lee Harvey Oswald's.

EXERCISE 8

Fill in the wh-question word and the correct form of be to complete each question.

Andrea: (1) <u>Where were</u> you on the day of Kennedy's assassination?

Helene: I was in school. There was an announcement over the loud speaker.

Andrea: (2) <u>Who were</u> you with at the time?

Helene: I was with my friend Patty.

Andrea: (3) <u>How was</u> it in school that day?

Helene: It was terrible. We were all very upset and silent.

Andrea: (4) <u>Why were</u> you all silent?

Helene: because it was hard to believe he was dead.

Andrea: And at home? (5) <u>How were</u> things at home?

Helene: At home, things were very bad. My parents were in shock too.

Andrea: (6) <u>How were</u> their feelings after the assassination?

Helene: They were angry, sad, confused, and afraid.

Look at the photo and write a *wh*-question for each answer.

1. _who were these people?_ ?

These people were mountain climbers.

2. _where were they?_ ?

They were in the Himalayas.

3. _why were they there?_ ?

They were there for the adventure and the challenge.

4. _when were they there?_ ?

They were there in 1996.

5. _what was the name?_ ?

The name of the mountain was Mount Everest.

6. _whose idea was it to take this trip?_ ?

It was their idea to take this trip.

7. _why was this trip bad?_ ?

The trip was a disaster; eight people died on this trip.

Work in a group. Take turns. One student makes a statement about last weekend. The other students ask questions. Use *wh*-questions and the past tense of *be*.

EXAMPLE: Statement: I was at the movies on Saturday.

   Questions: What was the movie? Who were you with?

   Who was in the movie? How was the movie?

Correct the mistakes in the following sentences.

1. Do was Indira Gandhi and Golda Meir Prime Minister? *were indira Gandhi and Golda ---*

2. The Beatles wasn't fashion designers. *weren't*

3. Was hot the weather at Disneyworld last week?

4. Where the earthquake was in Japan in 1996?

5. Why the people were on Mount Everest?

6. Was good the service at the restaurant? *weren't any dates in the opening task.*

7. No was any dates in the Opening Task. *There were no*

8. How it was the trip to Disneyworld?

Activities

ACTIVITY 1

Work with a partner, finish writing the story of Cinderella in Exercise 5 (page 262).

ACTIVITY 2

Work with a partner. Ask your partner the questions below and other questions to find out about a special place he or she knows.

QUESTIONS: Where were you last summer? When were you there?

   Why were you there? What was special about this place?

   How was the weather? Were the people friendly? How was the food?

ACTIVITY 3

With the information from Activity 1, tell the class about your partner's special place.

EXAMPLE: Last summer, my partner was in Greece. She was there with her boy-friend. Greece was very beautiful and interesting.

ACTIVITY 4

Work in a group.

STEP ❶ Write the dates below on pieces of paper. Mix all the papers together.

STEP ❷ Pick a piece of paper and say something about your life at that time and your life now. Take turns with the classmates in your group.

EXAMPLE: In 1995, I was a doctor in the Philippines, but now I am an ESL student in the United States.

July 1995	September 1996	December 1995
1994	1991	1993
1990	in the 1980s	1992
1970	1960	

ACTIVITY 5

 STEP ❶ Listen to the beginning of the stories on tape. Decide what kind of story type each one is. Write the number of the story you hear next to the story type.

A horror story _____   A murder mystery   _____

A love story _____   A children's story/fairy tale   _____

STEP ❷ Finish one of the stories. Tell the story to the class.

Past Tense

Solve the Mystery: Who took the VCR?

STEP ❶ Read the mystery.

For most students, Ms. Ditto was the best ESL teacher in the English Language Center. Three years ago, she began to use a VCR in her classes. She brought in interesting videotapes for her students to watch every week. The students enjoyed her classes and really liked her.

Only one student, Harry, didn't like Ms. Ditto. Harry's writing wasn't very good, so he failed Ms. Ditto's class twice. Last summer, he got a job in the language lab to pay the tuition for her class again this semester. Yes, Harry felt angry at Ms. Ditto.

Just before the new semester started, the Director of the English Language Center heard the university didn't have money to pay the teachers. They were not able to give Ms. Ditto a job this semester. Everyone was sad. Harry just laughed!

On the first day of class, Professor Brown wanted to use the VCR. He asked Harry to open the language lab. But when Harry opened the door to the lab, the VCR was not there. In its place, there was a typed note with a signature on it. The note said:

```
    Today, I very sad. I no can work in English Language
Center because there no have money to pay me. What I
can do now? How I can live? I take this VCR because I
have angry. Please understand my. I sorry . . .
```
                                                    C. Ditto

STEP ❷ Read the sentences and check True or False.

	True	False
1. Ms. Ditto's students didn't like her.		
2. Harry needed money.		
3. Harry worked in the language lab.		
4. Ms. Ditto didn't have a job this semester.		
5. Harry disliked Ms. Ditto.		
6. Harry did well in Ms. Ditto's class.		

STEP ❸ Solve the mystery. Discuss your answers with the class.

Who took the VCR? How do you know?

Spelling of Regular Past-Tense Verbs

SUBJECT	BASE FORM + -ED
I You He She It We You They	started three years ago.

Regular verbs can change spelling in the simple past tense.

IF THE VERB ENDS IN:	SPELLING RULE
(a) a consonant **want** **need**	Add -*ed* **wanted** **needed**
(b) a vowel + *y* **enjoy** **play**	Add -*ed* **enjoyed** **played**
(c) a consonant + *e* **like** **smile**	Add -*d* **liked** **smiled**
(d) a consonant + *y* **study** **worry**	Change -*y* to -*i*, add -*ed* **studied** **worried**
(e) consonant + vowel + consonant (one syllable verbs) **stop** **drop**	Double the consonant, add -*ed* **stopped** **dropped**
(f) -*x*, -*w* (one syllable verbs) **show** **fix**	Do not double the consonant, add -*ed* **showed** **fixed**
(g) two-syllable verbs stress on the last syllable **oCCUR** **preFER**	Double the consonant, add -*ed* **occurred** **preferred**
(h) two-syllable verbs stress on the first syllable **LISten** **VISit**	Do not double the consonant, add -*ed* **listened** **visited**

Go back to the Opening Task on page 270 and underline all the regular past-tense verbs in the mystery.

EXAMPLE: They <u>enjoyed</u> her classes and really <u>liked</u> her.

Fill in the blanks with the past tense of the verbs.

1. Ms. Ditto _enjoyed_ (enjoy) her classes.

2. Ms. Ditto _used_ (use) interesting videotapes in her classes.

3. She _helped_ (help) her students to understand the tapes.

4. The students _studied_ (study) new vocabulary.

5. They _learned_ (learn) about American life.

6. They _discussed_ (discuss) the tapes in class.

7. The students _played_ (play) language learning games in class.

8. Many students _registered_ (register) for her class every semester.

9. All the students really _loved_ (love) her.

10. Ms. Ditto _stopped_ (stop) teaching because the university didn't have money to pay her.

11. Ms. Ditto's students _cried_ (cry).

12. One day, a robbery _occurred_ (occur) at the English Language Center.

13. A VCR _disappeared_ (disappear) from the language lab.

disappeared.

ue oai

Pronunciation of the *-ed* Ending

VERB END	EXAMPLES
Group I After voiceless sounds*, the final *-ed* is pronounced /t/.	/t/ *asked* *kissed* *stopped*
Group II After voiced sounds**, the final *-ed* is pronounced /d/.	/d/ *robbed* *killed* *played*
Group III After /t/ and /d/, the final *-ed* is pronounced /ɪd/.	/ɪd/ *pointed* *wanted* *waited*

*Voiceless sounds: s, k, p, f, sh, ch, x.
**Voiced sound: b, g, l, m, n, r, v, z, or a vowel

EXERCISE 3

STEP ❶ Put each verb in the simple past and read each sentence aloud. Check the column that shows the pronunciation of each verb.

Bookworm Benny was an excellent student.

	/t/	/d/	/ɪd/
1. Teachers always ___liked___ (like) Bookworm Benny.	✔		
2. He _____ (work) hard in school.	✓		
3. He always _____ (finish) his work first.		✓	
4. The teacher always _____ (call) on him.		✓	
5. He always _____ (answer) questions correctly.		✓	

	/t/	/d/	/ɪd/
6. He _____ (remember) all his lessons.		✓	
7. He never _____ (talk) out of turn.	✓		
8. The other students _____ (hate) Benny.			✓
9. One day, they _____ (decide) to get him into trouble.			✓
10. They _____ (roll) a piece of paper into a ball.		✓	
11. They _____ (wait) for the teacher to turn his back.			✓
12. They threw the paper ball at the teacher. It _____ (land) on the teacher's head.			✓
13. The teacher was really angry. He _____ (yell) at the class.		✓	
14. "Who did that?" he _____ (ask).	✓		
15. All the students _____ (point) to Benny.			✓
16. But the teacher _____ (trust) Benny.			✓
17. The teacher _____ (punish) the other students.	✓		

STEP ❷ The pictures about Bookworm Benny are not in the correct order. Number the pictures in the correct order. Then use the pictures to retell Bookworm Benny's story.

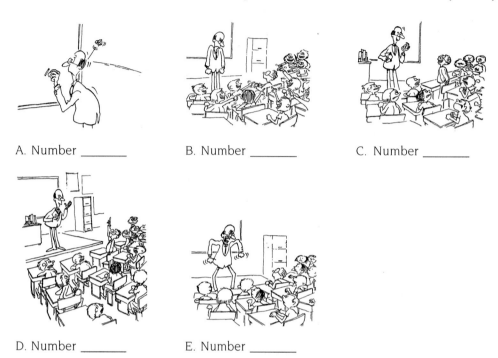

A. Number _____

B. Number _____

C. Number _____

D. Number _____

E. Number _____

EXERCISE 4

The solution to the Ms. Ditto story is in this exercise. Fill in the blanks with the past tense of the verbs in the box.

discuss	look	remember	fire	notice	learn
type	confess	believe	lock	ask	sign

When the Director of the English Language Center (1) __learned__ about the robbery, she was sad. She (2) _____ Ms. Ditto was an honest person.

To solve the mystery, the Director (3) _____ herself in her office alone. She (4) _____ the problems between Harry and Ms. Ditto. Then, the Director (5) _____ at the note again. She (6) _____ all the grammar mistakes! And the signature on the note was not Ms. Ditto's signature.

The Director (7) _____ Harry to come to her office. She (8) _____ the problem with him. Finally, Harry (9) _____ to the crime. Harry said, "I (10) _____ the note and

(11) _____ Ms. Ditto's name." In the end, the Director

(12) _____ Harry.

Irregular Past-Tense Verbs: Affirmative Statements

Many verbs in the past tense are irregular. They do not have the *-ed* form.

SUBJECT	VERB	
I You He She It We You They	went	to New York last year.

You can learn irregular past-tense forms in groups.

BASE FORM	SIMPLE PAST
/I/ sound	**/ae/ sound**
begin	began
drink	drank
ring	rang
sing	sang
sink	sank
swim	swam

BASE FORM	SIMPLE PAST
	ought/aught
buy	bought
bring	brought
catch	caught
fight	fought
teach	taught
think	thought

BASE FORM	SIMPLE PAST
	Base form and past-tense forms are the same
cost	cost
cut	cut
hit	hit
hurt	hurt
put	put
quit	quit
shut	shut
let	let
-ow	**-ew**
blow	blew
grow	grew
know	knew
throw	threw
/iy/ sound	**/ɜ/ sound**
feed	fed
feel	felt
keep	kept
lead	led
leave	left
meet	met
read	read
sleep	slept
-d	**-t**
lend	lent
send	sent
spend	spent
bend	bent
build	built

BASE FORM	SIMPLE PAST
	Change of vowel
become	became
come	came
dig	dug
draw	drew
fall	fell
forget	forgot
get	got
give	gave
hold	held
hang	hung
run	ran
sit	sat
win	won
	/o/ sound
break	broke
choose	chose
sell	sold
tell	told
speak	spoke
steal	stole
drive	drove
ride	rode
wake	woke
write	wrote

BASE FORM	SIMPLE PAST
	Other
be	was
bite	bit
do	did
eat	ate
find	found
fly	flew
go	went
have	had
hear	heard
hide	hid
lose	lost
make	made
pay	paid
say	said
see	saw
shake	shook
shoot	shot
stand	stood
take	took
tear	tore
understand	understood
wear	wore

(See Appendix 8 for an alphabetical list of common irregular past-tense verbs.)

EXERCISE 5

Go back to the Opening Task on page 270. Circle the irregular past-tense verbs.

EXAMPLE: For most students, Ms. Ditto (was) the best ESL teacher in the English Language Center.

EXERCISE 6

Liisa and Kate are from Finland. They had a dream vacation in New York last fall. Fill in the blanks with the past tense of the verbs in parentheses.

1. Liisa and Kate _flew_____ (fly) to New York on Sunday, November 4.

2. They _____ (find) many interesting things to do in the city.

3. They _____ (eat) great food every day.

4. They _____ (go) to the Statue of Liberty.

5. They _____ (take) a ferry to the Immigration Museum at Ellis Island.

6. They _____ (stand) at the top of the World Trade Center.

7. They _____ (spend) an evening at a jazz club.

8. Liisa _____ (buy) gifts for her friends in Finland.

9. They _____ (see) an exhibit at the Museum of Modern Art.

10. They _____ (meet) a nice woman at the museum.

11. They _____ (speak) English with her all afternoon.

12. They _____ (think) New York was a beautiful, friendly city.

EXERCISE 7

Monique and Daniel are from France. Their vacation in New York was a nightmare. Fill in the blanks with the past tense of the verbs in parentheses.

1. On Sunday, November 4, Monique and Daniel's flight to New York was late, so they _sat_____ (sit) in the airport for four hours.

2. The airline company _____ (lose) all their luggage, so on Monday they _____ (go) shopping for new clothes.

3. On Tuesday, they _____ (get) stuck in the subway when their train _____ (break) down.

4. On Wednesday, they _____ (pay) ninety dollars to rent a car, and _____ (drive) to the Aquarium.

5. They _____ (leave) the car on the street and _____ (get) a fifty-dollar parking ticket!

6. A thief _____ (throw) a rock through the car window and _____ (steal) Monique's camera.

7. On Thursday, they _____ (buy) a new camera downtown.

8. On Friday, they _____ (go) ice skating at Rockefeller Center. Monique had the new camera around her neck.

9. Monique _____ (fall) on the ice _____ (hurt) her knee.

10. She _____ (break) her new camera.

11. Monique was wet and frozen, so she _____ (catch) a cold.

12. On Saturday night, they _____ (eat) some unusual food in a restaurant.

13. On Sunday morning, they each _____ (wake) up with stomach problems.

14. Later that Sunday, they _____ (take) a taxi to the airport and finally _____ (leave) for home.

FOCUS 4 ▷▷▷▷▷▷▷▷▷▷▷▷▷ FORM/MEANING

Time Expressions

Time expressions tell us when the action occurred in the past.

yesterday morning afternoon evening	last night week month year summer	an hour ago two days six months a year	in 1988 on Sunday at 6:00 the day before yesterday

EXAMPLES	EXPLANATIONS
(a) **On Sunday,** they flew to New York. **(b)** Liisa and Kate went to Spain **two years ago.**	Time expressions can come at the beginning or at the end of a sentence.
(c) **Yesterday morning,** a VCR disappeared from the English Language Center.	Use a comma after the time expression if it is at the beginning of the sentence.

EXERCISE 8

Think back to Monique and Daniel's nightmare vacation in New York. Use time expressions to complete the sentences.

EXAMPLE: _Last_____ Sunday, Monique and Daniel left Paris for New York City.

1. Monique and Danielle left New York _____last_____ Sunday.

2. Their plane took off _____at_____ 8 o'clock _____in_____ the evening.

3. It is now Tuesday, November 13. Monique and Danielle are back in Paris. Monique and Danielle returned to Paris _____yesterday_____.

4. They left New York _____on Sunday_____.

5. _____last_____ week, they had bad luck every day.

6. It was exactly a week _____ that they got stuck on the subway in New York.

EXERCISE 9

Make true statements about yourself. Use each of the time expressions below.

EXAMPLE: Six months ago

Six months ago, _I took a trip to Mexico._____

1. Two months ago, _____

2. In 1988, _____

3. Last year, _____

4. Last summer, _____

5. Two days ago, _____

6. On Sunday, _____

7. The day before yesterday, _____

8. Yesterday morning, _____

9. At six o'clock this morning, _____

10. An hour ago, _____

FOCUS 5 ➤➤➤➤➤➤➤➤➤➤➤➤➤➤➤➤➤➤➤➤➤ FORM

Past Tense: Negative Statements

SUBJECT	DID + NOT DIDN'T	BASE FORM OF VERB
I You He She It We You They	**did not** **didn't**	work.

EXERCISE 10

Make affirmative or negative statements aloud about the people in this unit.

EXAMPLE: the teacher/like Benny   } affirmative.

The teacher liked Benny.

the teacher/get angry at Benny.

The teacher didn't get angry at Benny.   } negative.

1. The other students/like Bookworm Benny   + tried.   didn't try.
2. The teacher/trust Benny
3. The students/try to get Benny into trouble.
4. The students' plan for Benny/succeed
5. Liisa and Kate/lose their luggage
6. Liisa's camera/break
7. Liisa and Kate/get stuck on the subway
8. Liisa and Kate/enjoy their vacation in New York
9. Harry/notice the grammar mistakes in his note
10. Ms. Ditto/sign the note

11. Harry/steal the VCR

12. The Director/believe Harry

13. Monique and Daniel/spend an evening at a jazz club

14. Monique and Daniel/visit the United Nations

15. Monique and Daniel/enjoy their vacation in New York

 FOCUS 6 >>>>>>>>>>>>>>>>>>>>>>>>> **FORM**

Past Tense: Yes/No Questions and Short Answers

Yes/No Questions

DID	SUBJECT	BASE FORM OF THE VERB	
Did	I you he she we you they	visit	New York last year?

Short Answers

AFFIRMATIVE			NEGATIVE		
Yes,	I you he she we you they	did.	No,	I you he she we you they	did not. didn't.

Ask a partner *yes/no* questions about the mystery story.

EXAMPLES: **Q:** understand the mystery

Did you understand the mystery?

A: Yes, I did.

1. like the Ms. Ditto story
2. enjoy being a detective
3. think Ms. Ditto took the VCR
4. guess that Harry was the thief
5. find the grammar mistakes in Harry's note
6. correct the mistakes in the note
7. feel sorry for Harry
8. want to give Harry any advice

Look at the cartoon about Jerry, a man with very bad luck. He went on a two-week cruise last winter and there was a big storm at sea.

STEP ❶ Ask a partner *yes/no* questions with the words below. The pictures can help you answer the questions.

EXAMPLE: Jerry/go on a cruise last winter

Did Jerry go on a cruise last winter?

Yes, he did.

1. Jerry's ship/reach its destination
2. Jerry/know how to swim
3. Jerry/die
4. he/find an island
5. he/meet anyone on the island
6. the island/have stores
7. he/have enough food
8. he/write postcards home
9. he/make tools
10. he/build a good boat

STEP ❷ Remember, Jerry has very bad luck. Ask each other Yes/No questions and guess the end of the story. See the Appendix for the conclusion to Exercise 12 (page E-4).

11. Jerry's luck/change
12. a helicopter/find Jerry
13. Jerry/find his way back home
14. the story/have a happy ending
15. Jerry/ever take another cruise again

FOCUS 7 ➤➤➤➤➤➤➤➤➤➤➤➤➤➤➤➤➤➤➤➤➤➤ **FORM**

Past Tense: *Wh*-Questions

WH-WORD	DID	SUBJECT	BASE FORM OF VERB	ANSWERS
What **When**		I you	do last summer? make plans?	You went to Paris. (I made plans) last month.
Where		he	go last summer?	(He went) to Scotland.
Why		the ship	sink?	(It sank) because there was a storm.
How	**did**	she	get to Paris?	(She got there) by plane.
How long		they	stay in New York?	(They stayed there for) two weeks.
How long ago		you	visit Alaska?	(I visited Alaska) ten years ago.
Who(m)		Liisa and Kate	meet in New York?	(They met) a nice woman.

WH-WORD AS SUBJECT	PAST TENSE VERB	ANSWERS
What	happened to Jerry's ship?	It sank.
Who	had a terrible vacation?	Monique and Daniel.

EXERCISE 13

Write Wh-questions about Jerry. Then ask your partner the questions. Your partner gives an answer or says "I don't know."

EXAMPLE: Jerry/eat on the island?

     Q: What _did Jerry eat on the island_ _____ ?

     A: _(He ate) fruit from the trees and fish from the sea._ _____

1. Jerry/go on vacation

   Q: Where _____ ?

   A: _____

2. Jerry/go on vacation

   Q: When _____ ?

   A: _____

3. Jerry/leave home

   Q: How long ago _____ ?

   A: _____

4. Jerry's ship/sink

   Q: Why _____ ?

   A: _____

5. Jerry/do after the ship sank

   Q: What _____ ?

   A: _____

6. Jerry/meet on the island

   Q: Who(m) _____ ?

   A: _____

7. Jerry/build the boat

   Q: How _____?

   A: _____

8. Jerry/put on the boat

   Q: What _____?

   A: _____

9. Jerry/feel when he finished the boat

   Q: How _____?

   A: _____

10. the story end

   Q: How _____?

   A: _____

EXERCISE 14

Make questions that ask for the underlined information. Use *who*, *whom*, or *what*.

EXAMPLE: Q: _What did the students enjoy_ _____?

      A: The students enjoyed <u>Ms. Ditto's classes.</u>

1: **Q:** _____?

   A: The students loved <u>Ms. Ditto.</u>

2: **Q:** _____?

   A: Ms. Ditto used <u>a VCR</u> in her classes.

3: **Q:** _____?

   A: Harry wanted to hurt <u>Ms. Ditto.</u>

4: **Q:** _____?

   A: <u>Harry</u> got hurt in the end.

5: **Q:** _____?

   A: <u>Professor Brown</u> found the note.

6: **Q:** _____?

   A: <u>The Director</u> fired Harry.

7: **Q:** _____?

  A: Harry stole <u>the VCR</u>.

8: **Q:** _____?

  A: The Director fired <u>Harry</u>.

9: **Q:** _____?

  A: The moral of the story was "<u>crime doesn't pay</u>."

EXERCISE 15

Information Gap B. This is a story about a very special woman named Doina. Work with a partner. You look at Text A, and ask questions to get the information for the sentences with the blanks. Your partner looks at Text B on page E-4, and asks questions to get the information for the blanks in Text B.

  EXAMPLE: Your Partner: (Look at Text B)   1. Where did Doina grow up?

  You: (Look at Text A)   1. She grew up in Romania.

TEXT A:

1. Doina grew up in Romania.

2. She married _____ (who/m)

3. She had a daughter in 1976.

4. Doina was unhappy because she was against the government in Romania.

5. She thought of _____ (what) every day.

6. She taught her daughter how to swim.

7. On October 9, 1988, she and her daughter swam across the Danube River. They swam to _____ (where)

8. The police caught them.

9. Doina and her daughter went _____ (where)

10. They tried to escape several months later.

11. Finally, they left Romania _____ (how)

12. They flew to New York in 1989.

13. Doina went to school _____ (why)

14. She wrote the story of her escape from Romania in her ESL class.

Correct the mistakes in the following sentences.

1. This morning, I waked up early.
2. I saw him yesterday night.
3. Harry didn't felt sad.
4. They don't met the Mayor of New York last week.
5. What Harry wanted?
6. Harry didn't noticed his mistakes.
7. Who did signed the note?
8. What did the Director?
9. What did happen to Harry?
10. Where Liisa and Kate went on vacation?
11. Who did go with Lisa to New York?
12. How Jerry built a boat?
13. They no had dinner in a Greek restaurant.
14. Whom did trust the teacher in the Bookworm Benny story?
15. The ship sank before a long time.

Activities

ACTIVITY 1

STEP ❶ Get into groups. One person in the group thinks of a famous person from the past.

STEP ❷ The others in the group can ask up to twenty *yes/no* questions to guess who the person is. After twenty questions the group loses if they haven't guessed.

    EXAMPLE: Did this person sing?

               Did this person live in North America?

               Was this person a woman?

Write your own ending for the story about Jerry. Compare your ending with your class-mates'. Who has the best ending? When you are finished, look at the cartoons that tell the end of Jerry's story on page E-4. How does your ending compare with the ending in the cartoon?

ACTIVITY 3

Work in groups of three.

STEP ❶ Each person tells a true personal story. The group chooses one story. Then each of you learns as much as you can about that story.

STEP ❷ Each of you tells the same beginning to the class. Your classmates ask each of you questions to find out who is telling the truth. Your job is to make the class believe this is your story.

> **EXAMPLE: Student 1 says:** When I was ten years old, I went on a long trip.
>
> **Student 2 says:** When I was ten years old, I went on a long trip.
>
> **Student 3 says:** When I was ten years old, I went on a long trip.
>
> **The Class asks:** Where did you go?
>
> Who(m) did you go with? etc.

ACTIVITY 4

Interview a partner about a past vacation. Ask as many *wh*-questions as you can. Report back to the class about your partner's trip.

> **EXAMPLE:** Where did you go?   How long did you stay?
>
> When did you go?   With whom did you go?
>
> How did you get there?   Why did you go there?
>
> What did you do there?

STEP ❶ Listen to the three students talking about their vacations. Match the students to the titles of the essays they wrote about their vacations.

Names	Essay Titles
Pedro	A Great Vacation
Hakim	My Terrible Trip
Angela	A Boring Vacation

STEP ❷ In a group discuss why each vacation was good or bad. What is your opinion of each vacation?

ACTIVITY 6

Jeopardy Game. Your teacher will choose one student to be the host. Only the host can look at the complete game board (page E-5). The rest of the class will be divided into two teams. Team 1 chooses a category and an amount of money from the game board. The host reads the answer. Team 1 has one minute to ask a correct question. If Team 1 can't, Team 2 gets a chance to ask a question. There can be more than one correct question for each answer. The team with the most money wins.

EXAMPLE: Team 1 chooses: People for $10.

Host reads: Ms. Ditto

Team 1 asks: Who lost her job?

Who(m) did Harry hate?

GAME BOARD

$$$	Category 1 PEOPLE	Category 2 WH-QUESTIONS	Category 3 YES/NO QUESTIONS
$10 $20 $30 $40 $50			

ACTIVITY 7

The stories in this unit are about unfair or unlucky things that happen to people. Think about a time when something unfair or unlucky happened to you. Write your story and tell the class what happened. Your classmates can ask you questions.

19 Reflexive Pronouns, Reciprocal Pronoun: *Each Other*

Advice Columns

STEP ❶ Read the letters to "Dear Darcy" in Part A. Match each one to a "Letter of Advice" in Part B. Fill in the name of the person who wrote each letter in the blanks in Part B.

PART A

Dear Darcy,

I'm married and have two children. I'm trying to be a super-woman. I do all of the housework, shopping, and the cleaning. I help my children with their school work. I never have time for myself. I am tired and unhappy. Please help!

—*Supermom in Seattle*

Dear Darcy,

My wife and I never go out anymore. We have a new baby, and my wife doesn't want to get a baby sitter. I'm starting to talk to myself! Can you help me?

—*Bored in Boston*

Dear Darcy,

My mom and dad got divorced last month. They fought with each other a lot, and finally, my dad moved out. Maybe I wasn't a good daughter to them. Maybe the break-up was my fault. What do you think?

—*Guilty in Gainesville*

PART B

A. Dear _____,

   Don't blame yourself. You did not cause the problems. This is your parents' problem.

B. Dear _____,

   You need to explain how you feel to her. Tell her you want to go out once a week. Life is short. Go out and enjoy yourselves!

C. Dear _____,

   You need to make time for yourself. Go out with your friends. Do yourself a favor and join a gym. Take care of yourself too. Buy yourself something special.

STEP ❷ Read the last letter from *Lonely in Los Angeles*. Circle the correct pronouns in Darcy's answer.

Dear Darcy:

   I'm a rather shy and lonely high school student. I'm doing well in school, but I don't have many friends. The girls in my class always call each other, but they never call me. I don't go out. I don't enjoy myself. I don't even like myself very much anymore.

                                                                    Lonely in Los Angeles

Dear Lonely in Los Angeles:

   Remember, the teenage years are difficult. At 16, many girls don't like (they/them/themselves). You're doing well in school. Be proud of (you/yourself). Try to like (you/yourself) first. Then others will like (you/yourself). Teenage girls need (each other/themselves). Force (you/yourself) to open up to other girls. Relax and try to enjoy (you/yourself).

                                                                    Darcy

FOCUS 1 >>>>>>>>>>>>>>>>>>>>>>>>>> FORM

Reflexive Pronouns

past happiness : hạnh phúc đã qua; hạnh phúc ② quá khứ

Use a reflexive pronoun when the subject and object are the same.

EXAMPLE: Sara bought **herself** a new car.

NOT: Sara bought Sara a new car.

EXAMPLES	REFLEXIVE PRONOUNS
(a) I bought **myself** a new car.	*myself*
(b) Look at **yourself** in the mirror.	*yourself*
(c) He doesn't take care of **himself.**	*himself*
(d) She blames **herself** for the accident.	*herself*
(e) A cat licks **itself** to keep clean.	*itself*
(f) We enjoyed **ourselves** at the theater.	*ourselves*
(g) Help **yourselves** to some food.	*yourselves*
(h) Babies can't feed **themselves.**	*themselves*

EXERCISE 1

Go back to the Opening Task on page 293. Underline all the reflexive pronouns and the subjects.

EXAMPLE: I never have time for myself.

EXERCISE 2

Fill in each blank with a reflexive pronoun.

EXAMPLE: I lost my wallet yesterday, and I wanted to kick **myself**.

1. **Mary:** Do you sometimes talk to _____?

   Bill: Well, sometimes, when I'm alone.

2. **Monica:** Thanks for such a lovely evening. We really enjoyed (a) _____.

   Gloria: Well, thanks for coming. And the children were just wonderful. They really behaved (b) _____ all evening. I hope you can come back soon.

3. **Jane:** I can't believe my bird flew out the window! It's my fault. I forgot to close the birdcage.

   Margaret: Don't blame _____. He's probably happier now. He's free.

4. **Cynthia:** What's the matter with Bobby's leg?

   Enrique: He hurt _____ at the soccer game last night.

5. **Jason:** My girlfriend Judy really knows how to take care of _____. She eats well, exercises regularly, and gets plenty of sleep.

6. **Sylvia:** Hello Carol, hello Eugene. Come on in. Make (a) _____ at home. Help (b) _____ to some drinks.

7. **Mother:** Be careful! that pot on the stove is very hot. Don't burn _____.

FOCUS 2 >>>>>>>>>>>>>>>> MEANING/USE

Verbs Commonly Used with Reflexive Pronouns/*By* + Reflexive Pronoun

EXAMPLES	EXPLANATIONS
(a) I fell and **hurt myself.** (b) He **taught himself** to play the guitar. (c) Be careful! Don't **cut yourself** with that knife. (d) Did you **enjoy yourself** at the party?	These verbs are commonly used with reflexive pronouns: *hurt* *cut* *tell* *burn* *blame* *enjoy* *teach* *introduce* *behave* *take care of*
(e) He got up, washed, and shaved.	The verbs *wash*, *dress*, and *shave* do not usually take reflexive pronouns. In sentence (e) it is clear he washed and shaved himself and not another person.
(f) He's only two, but he wants to get dressed **by himself.** (g) I sometimes go to the movies **by myself.**	Use *by* + a reflexive pronoun to show that someone is doing something alone (without company or help).

Write a sentence with a reflexive pronoun for each picture.

EXAMPLE: *The woman is introducing herself to the man.*

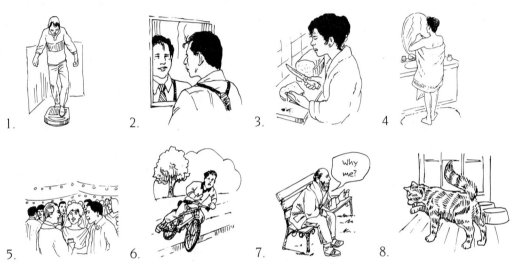

1. 2. 3. 4

5. 6. 7. 8.

cut	dry	enjoy	look at/admire
clean/lick	hurt	talk to	weigh

1. _____

2. _____

3. _____

4. _____

5. _____

6. _____

7. _____

8. _____

Reciprocal Pronoun: *Each Other*

The reciprocal pronoun *each other* is different in meaning from a reflexive pronoun.

(a) John and Ann blamed **themselves** for the accident.

(b) John and Ann blamed **each other** for the accident.

EXERCISE 4

Work with a partner. Draw pictures to show the differences in meaning between the following sentences.

1. **(a)** The weather was very hot. The runners poured water on themselves after the race.

   (b) The weather was very hot. The runners poured water on each other after the race.

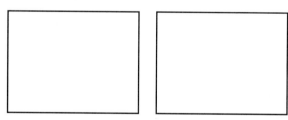

2. **(a)** They love themselves.

   (b) They love each other.

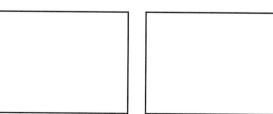

Act out the following sentences to show the difference between *each other* and reflexive pronouns.

1. You and your classmate are looking at yourselves in the mirror.
2. You and your classmate are looking at each other.
3. You and your classmate are talking to yourselves.
4. You and your classmate are talking to each other.
5. You're playing ball with a friend, and you break a neighbor's window. Blame yourself for the accident.
6. You're playing ball with a friend, and you break a neighbor's window. Blame each other for the accident.
7. You introduce yourself to your partner.
8. You and your partner introduce each other to a third person.

Choose a reflexive pronoun or *each other* to complete the statements.

1. An egotistical person loves _himself/herself_____.
2. Divorced people can be friends if they forgive _____.
3. Good friends protect _____.
4. Close friends tell _____ their secrets.
5. A self-confident person believes in _____.
6. In a good relationship, the two people trust _____.
7. A realistic person doesn't lie to _____.
8. Independent people take care of _____.
9. Caring people help _____.
10. Angry people say things to hurt _____.
11. Young children can't always control _____.
12. An insecure person doesn't have confidence in _____.

Circle the correct word in the "Dear Darcy" letters below.

EXAMPLE: ((He,) Him, Himself) cares about (I, (me,) myself).

Dear Darcy,

(1) (I, My, Mine) boyfriend loves himself. (2) (He, His, Him) is very pleased with (3) (he, him, himself). He always looks at (4) (he, him, himself) in store windows when he passes by. (5) (Himself, He, Him) only thinks about (6) (his, himself, him). He never brings (7) (my, me, myself) flowers. The last time he told (8) (my, me, myself) that he loved me was two years ago. He's also very selfish with (9) (he, his, him) things. For example, he never lends me (10) (him, himself, his) car. He says that the car is (11) (himself, him, his), and he doesn't want me to use it. Do (12) (yourself, your, you) have any advice for me?

"Unhappy"

Dear Unhappy:

(13) (You, Your, Yourself) boyfriend is very selfish. (14) (You, Your, Yourself) can't really change (15) (he, himself, him). Get rid of (16) (he, himself, him)! Find (17) (you, yourself, yours) a new guy!

Darcy

Correct the mistakes in the following sentences.

1. I hurt me.

2. They're looking at theirselves in the mirror.

3. I shave myself every morning.

4. I have a friend in Poland. We write to ourselves every month.

5. We enjoyed at the circus.

6. Larry blamed Harry for the accident. Harry blamed Larry for the accident. They blamed themselves for the accident.

7. He did it hisself.

Activities

ACTIVITY 1

Read the following riddle and try to find the answer. Discuss it with a partner. The answer is on page AK-1.

A prison guard found a prisoner hanging from a rope in his prison cell. Did he hang himself or did someone murder him? There was nothing else in the prison cell but a puddle of water on the floor.

ACTIVITY 2

Who is the most independent person in your class?

Make up a survey with ten questions. Then go around to all the students in your class and ask your questions. Tell the class who the independent people are.

EXAMPLE: Do you like to do things by yourself?

Do you usually travel by yourself?

Do you ever go to the movies by yourself?

ACTIVITY 3

Interview another classmate, using the questions below.

1. Do you believe in yourself?

2. When you go shopping for clothes, do you like to look at yourself in the mirror?

3. Do you ever compare yourself to other people?

4. Do you ever buy yourself a present?

5. In a new relationship, do you talk about yourself or try to learn about the other person?

6. Do you ever talk to yourself?

7. Do you cook for yourself?

8. Do you blame yourself for your problems or do you blame others?

9. Do you take care of yourself? (Do you eat well? Do you get enough sleep?)

10. Do you ever get angry at yourself?

Add questions of your own.

ACTIVITY 4

Listen to the people talk about their problems.

STEP ❶ Match the problems to the people.

Person #1	_____	(a) Serious
Person #2	_____	(b) Lonely
Person #3	_____	(c) Unhealthy

STEP ❷ What advice can you give to each of these people? Tell your classmates.

Future Time
Will and *Be Going To, May* and *Might*

Looking into Wanda's Crystal Ball

What is Wanda the Fortune-teller saying about each person? Match the phrases to the correct person (or people). Then, make a statement about each person's future.

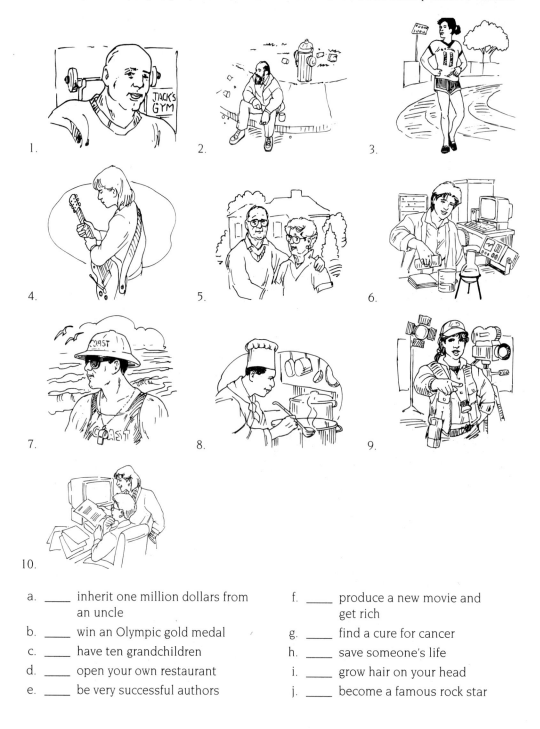

a. _____ inherit one million dollars from an uncle

b. _____ win an Olympic gold medal

c. _____ have ten grandchildren

d. _____ open your own restaurant

e. _____ be very successful authors

f. _____ produce a new movie and get rich

g. _____ find a cure for cancer

h. _____ save someone's life

i. _____ grow hair on your head

j. _____ become a famous rock star

FOCUS 1 ▷▷▷▷▷▷▷▷▷▷▷▷▷▷▷▷ MEANING/USE

Talking about Future Time

Use *will* and *be going to* to make predictions about the future or to say what you think will happen in the future.

EXAMPLES	EXPLANATIONS
(a) One day, he **will** be rich.	Use *will* for a prediction (what we think will happen).
(b) Look at those big black clouds. It **is going to** rain. NOT: It will rain.	Use *be going to* for a prediction based on the present situation (what we can see is going to happen).
(c) Teacher to student: Your parents **will** be very upset about this.	*Will* is more formal.
(d) Father to daughter: Your mother**'s going to** be very angry about this.	*Be going to* is less formal.

EXERCISE 1

Match the sentences to the pictures.

1.   2.   3.   4.

5.   6.   7.

a. _____ Look at that waiter! He's going to fall! d. _____ She's going to get a headache.

b. _____ This marriage isn't going to last. e. _____ I will always love you.

c. _____ You will find gold on the streets of f. _____ You will grow up and be famous!
America! g. _____ Be careful, Julian. You're going to fall.

FOCUS 2 ➤➤➤➤➤➤➤➤➤➤➤➤➤➤➤➤➤➤➤➤➤➤➤ **FORM**

Will

AFFIRMATIVE STATEMENTS		NEGATIVE STATEMENTS	
I You He She It We You They	**will arrive** next week. **'ll arrive** next week.	I You He She It We You They	**will not arrive** next week. **won't arrive** next week.
There	**will be** peace in the world. **'ll be**	There **will not be** any wars. **won't be**	
Men **will be able** to have babies.		Men **will not be** **able to** have babies. **won't**	

YES/NO QUESTIONS		SHORT ANSWERS					
Will	I you he she it we you they	arrive next week?	Yes,	you I he she it we you they	**will.**	No,	you I he she it we you they	**won't.**

WH-QUESTIONS	ANSWERS
(a) **When will** the scientists discover a cure?	(They **will discover** a cure) in ten years.
(b) **Where will** the couple go on their honeymoon?	(They **will go**) to Hawaii.
(c) **What will** the homeless man do with the money?	He**'ll buy** a new house.
(d) **How will** the couple travel?	(They**'ll travel**) by plane.
(e) **How** long **will** they be on the plane?	(They**'ll be** on the plane) for five hours.
(f) **Who will** get an Olympic medal?	The athlete.
(g) **Who(m) will** the lifeguard save?	(He**'ll save**) a lucky person.

EXERCISE 2

Think about the people in the Opening Task on page 304. Try to remember the predictions for each person. Say the prediction aloud.

EXAMPLE: The scientist *will find a cure for cancer.*

1. The bald man . . .
2. The athlete . . .
3. The teenager . . .
4. The movie director . . .
5. The lifeguard . . .
6. The chef . . .
7. The homeless man . . .
8. The authors . . .
9. The elderly couple . . .

How will our lives be different in fifty years? Make predictions with *will* or *won't*. Discuss your predictions with a partner.

1. The climate _____ change.

2. Pollution _____ be under control.

3. People _____ take vacations on the moon.

4. There _____ be few fish left in the oceans.

5. All countries _____ share the world's money equally.

6. Most people _____ move back to the countryside.

7. The traditional family with a husband, wife, and two children _____ disappear.

8. Men and women _____ continue to marry.

9. People of different races _____ learn to live together peacefully.

10. People _____ speak the same language.

11. Crime _____ stop.

12. People _____ drive electric cars.

13. We _____ discover life on other planets.

14. Science _____ continue to be very important.

15. People _____ live to be 130 years old.

16. A woman _____ be President of the United States.

Think about the year 2025. Where will you be? What will you be able to do? Write *yes/no* questions with *will*. Interview your classmates and report their answers to the class.

	Classmate 1	Classmate 2
1. be in the United States	_____	_____
Will you be in the United States?		
2. speak English fluently	_____	_____
3. be back in the country you come from	_____	_____

4. have a good job

      _____   _____

5. earn a living

      _____   _____

6. take care of a family

      _____   _____

7. have a nice house

      _____   _____

8. be content

      _____   _____

9. want something different

      _____   _____

Add two questions of your own.

10. _____   _____   _____

11. _____   _____   _____

EXERCISE 5

Work with a partner. You are Janice Williams and your partner is Wanda the Fortune-teller. Ask your partner *yes/no* and *wh*-questions with *will* and *will be able to*. Your partner looks into the crystal ball to answer your questions.

EXAMPLE: You: Will my husband lose his job?

        Your Partner: Yes, he will.

Wanda's Crystal Ball

Janice's Questions

1. my husband/lose his job?
2. my husband/be able to find another job?
3. when/my husband/find another job?
4. my daughter/get married?
5. who(m)/she/marry?
6. I/have grandchildren?
7. how many grandchildren/I/have?
8. my son/go to college?
9. what/he/do?
10. my husband and I/be able to retire?
11. where/we/retire?

Be Going To

AFFIRMATIVE STATEMENTS		NEGATIVE STATEMENTS	
I	**am** / **'m**		I	**am not** / **'m not**	
You	**are** / **'re**		You	**are not** / **aren't**	
He She It	**is** / **'s**	**going to** leave.	He She It	**is not** / **isn't**	**going to** leave.
We You They	**are** / **'re**		We You They	**are not** / **aren't**	

YES/NO QUESTIONS		SHORT ANSWERS				
Am	I			you	**are.**		you	**aren't.**
Are	you			I	**am.**		I'm	**not.**
Is	he she it	**going to** leave?	Yes,	he she it	**is.**	No,	he she it	**isn't.**
Are	we you they			we you they	**are.**		we you they	**aren't.**

WH-QUESTIONS			ANSWERS	
When		leave?		leave in two weeks.
Where		go?		go to Colorado.
What	**are you going to**	do there?	**I'm going to**	go skiing.
How		get there?		go by car.
How long		stay?		stay for one week.
Who(m)		visit?		visit my cousin.
Who**'s**	**going to**	drive?	My friend (is going to drive).	

Remember: *Going to* is often pronounced "gonna" when we speak. We do not usually write "gonna."

EXERCISE 6

Look at the pictures. Then fill in the blanks with the affirmative or negative form of *be going to*.

1. "Watch out! That bag _____ fall!"

2. "Hurry up! We _____ miss the bus."

3. "This _____ hurt you."

4. "I am so tired! I _____ take a nap."

5. "Hello, dear. I _____ be home on time tonight."

6. **George:** What are you _____ to have, Fred?
   Fred: I _____ to have a pizza, as usual.

7. "Watch her, Jack! She _____ fall into the pool!"

9. "They _____ have a baby."

10. "Hello, boss. I'm sorry, I _____ be able to come in today. I have a terrible backache and I can't get out of bed."

11. **Ben:** I have a test tomorrow. I _____ to study.

   Roommate: I have a test tomorrow too, but I _____ study. I _____ to watch the game on TV!

Read the answers. Write a *yes/no* or *wh*-question with *be going to*.

Richard: My doctor says I need to leave my job and get away somewhere.

Robert: (1) _Where are you going to go?_ ?

Richard: To California.

Robert: (2) _____ ?

Richard: I don't know (what I'm going to do there).

Robert: (3) _____ ?

Richard: (I'm going to stay) with some old friends.

Robert: (4) _____ ?

Richard: For about a month.

Robert: (5) _____ ?

Richard: By plane.

Robert: (6) _____ ?

Richard: I don't know (if I'm going to come back to my job).

Use your imagination to answer these questions about the people in the Opening Task on page 304. Use *be going to* in writing your answers. Compare your answers with your classmates'.

1. What is going to happen to the elderly people?

   They're going to live to a ripe old age.

2. What is the poor person going to do with the million dollars?

3. Who is the lifeguard going to save?

4. What kind of movie is the director going to make?

5. What kind of food is the chef going to have in his restaurant?

6. How are the authors going to celebrate their success?

7. What is the athlete going to do after the Olympics?

8. What kind of life is the rock star going to have?

FOCUS 4 ➤➤➤➤➤➤➤➤➤➤➤➤➤ **FORM/MEANING**

Time Expressions

EXAMPLES	EXPLANATIONS
(a) I'm going to visit you **tomorrow evening.** **(b)** **A month from now,** Wanda will be on a tropical island.	Future time expressions can come at the beginning or at the end of the sentence. Put a comma (,) after the time expression when it is at the beginning of the sentence.

Future Time Expressions

(Later) this	morning
	 afternoon
	 evening
		next	week
			 month
			 year
			 Sunday
			 weekend
				tomorrow	morning
					 afternoon
					 evening
					 night
						soon
						 later
						 the day after
						    tomorrow
						 a week from
						    today
						 tonight

EXAMPLES				EXPLANATIONS
I'll see you	**(c)**	**in**	fifteen minutes two weeks. March. 2015.	We also use prepositions of time to talk about future time.
	(d)	**on**	Tuesday May 21st.	
	(e)	**at**	4:00 midnight.	
(f) We are going to go to the Bahamas **for** three weeks.				*For* shows how long the action will last.
(g) I'll be there **until** 3:00. (At 3:00, I will leave. I will not be there after 3:00.) **(h)** I won't be there **until** Monday. (Before Monday, I won't be there. After Monday, I'll be there.)				*Until* shows the specific time in the future when the action will change.

EXERCISE 9

Make statements about yourself. Use *be going to*.

EXAMPLE: In a few days, I'm going to call my parents   .

1. In a few days, _____ .

2. Next summer, _____ .

3. The day after tomorrow, _____ .

4. This evening, _____ .

5. Tomorrow night, _____ .

6. This weekend, _____ .

7. At 9:00, _____ .

8. In December, _____ .

9. On Wednesday night, _____ .

Anthony and Sally are planning a vacation in Europe. They are going to visit four countries in seven days. Sally is telling Anthony about their travel plans. Fill in the blanks with *in, on, at, for,* or *until.*

1. We are going to arrive in London (a) __at__ 6:00 P.M.
   (b) __on__ Sunday.

2. We'll stay in London _____ two days.

3. Then, we'll fly to Paris _____ Tuesday morning.

4. We'll stay in Paris _____ Wednesday afternoon.

5. Then, we'll fly to Rome _____ the evening.

6. We won't leave Rome _____ Friday morning.

7. _____ 10:00 A.M. on Friday morning, we'll fly to our final destination, Athens, Greece.

8. We'll stay in Greece _____ two days.

9. We'll return home _____ Sunday. Then, we'll need a vacation!

Look at Wanda's calendar. Imagine it is now 2 p.m. on Wednesday, April 10, 1996. Read the sentences about Wanda's plans and fill in the blanks with a time expression or a preposition of time. There may be more than one correct answer.

SUNDAY	MONDAY	TUESDAY	WEDNESDAY	THURSDAY	FRIDAY	SATURDAY
APRIL	1	2	3	4	5	6
7	8	9	10 Last client 6:00 pm	11 polish crystal ball	12 deposit money in bank	13
14	15	16 buy new fortune cards	17	18 secretary goes on vacation	19 Fortune Teller's conference	20
21	22	23	24	25	26	27
28	29	30	31			

Still To Do:
First Edition of "How to Make Predictions" magazine arrives on June 10th
—Retire 2015!
—Write autobiography 2020

SUNDAY	MONDAY	TUESDAY	WEDNESDAY	THURSDAY	FRIDAY	SATU
MAY			1	2	3	4
5	6 place ad in newspaper	7	8	9	10	11
12	13	14				

1. Wanda is going to see her last client _at 6:00 this evening; in four hours_ .

2. She's going to attend the Fortune-tellers' Conference _____.

3. She's going to polish her crystal ball _____.

4. She's going to deposit all her money in the bank _____.

5. Her secretary is going to go on vacation _____.

6. She is going to buy new fortune cards _____.

7. She's going to put an advertisement about herself in the newspaper

   _____.

8. She will receive her first *How To Make Predictions* magazine

   _____.

9. She will retire to a tropical island _____.

10. She will write a book called *How to Be a Successful Fortune-teller in 10 Easy Lessons*

   _____.

FOCUS 5 >>>>>>>>>>>>>>>>>>>>>>>> **USE**

Talking about Future Intentions or Plans

EXAMPLES	EXPLANATIONS
(a) A: The phone is ringing. **B:** O.K. **I'll get** it.	Use *will* when you decide to do something at the time of speaking.
(b) Mother: Where are you going? Daughter: **I'm going to** take a drive with Richard tonight. Remember, Mom? You said it was okay . . . Mother: I did?	Use *going to* when you made a plan to do something before the time of speaking.

Work with a partner. You read the first five statements in Column A aloud. Your partner chooses an answer from Column B. After the first five, your partner reads from Column A and you choose the answer from Column B.

EXAMPLE: Do you have any plans for tonight?

   (B.) Yes, we're going to the theater.

Column A

1. Christine called. She's coming over for dinner.

2. What are you doing with that camera?

3. Do you need a ride home today?

4. We don't have a thing to eat in the house.

5. Help! The car died again.

6. Why are you meeting Jenny in the library tonight?

7. Look, those thieves are robbing the bank!

8. Mom, can you brush my hair?

9. Are you off the phone yet?

10. Why did Maria cancel her date for Saturday night?

Column B

A. Great! I'll cook.
B. Great! I'm going to cook.

A. I'll take your picture.
B. I'm going to take your picture.

A. No, thanks. Jason will take me home.
B. No, thanks. Jason's going to take me home.

A. I'll call up and order a pizza.
B. I'm going to call up and order a pizza.

A. Calm down. I'll be right there.
B. Calm down. I'm going to be right there.

A. She'll help me with my homework.
B. She's going to help me with my home work.

A. I'll call the police.
B. I'm going to call the police.

A. I'll do it in a minute, sweetie.
B. I'm going to do it in a minute, sweetie.

A. I'll be off in a minute!
B. I'm going to be off in a minute!

A. Her parents will take her away for the weekend.
B. Her parents are going to take her away for the weekend.

May and Might

Use *may* or *might* to say something is possible in the future.

EXAMPLES	EXPLANATIONS
(a) I **will go** to Mexico next year.	(a) shows certainty. The speaker is 100% sure.
(b) I **may/might go** to Mexico next year.	(b) shows possibility.

AFFIRMATIVE STATEMENTS			NEGATIVE STATEMENTS		
I You He She We You They	**may** **might**	study abroad next year. be able to stay abroad for two years.	I You He She We You They	**may not** **might not**	take a vacation. be able to stay for two years.
It		rain later.	It		rain later.
There		be cheap flights to Mexico.	There		be any discounts on flights.

NOTE:
- You cannot use *may* or *might* in *yes/no* questions.
- There are no contractions for *may* or *might*.

Either *may* or *might* is possible in the blanks. Fill in the blanks with *may* or *might* in the affirmative or negative.

EXAMPLE: Peter: How are you going to go to Boston next weekend?

Al: I _may_ drive or I _may_ take the train. I won't fly because it's expensive.

1. **Joanne:** Is Ilene going to come to your New Year's Eve party?

   Paula: She (a) _____ be able to come. She went out of town on business and she (b) _____ be back in time for the party.

2. **Tamara:** Where are you and Chip going to go on vacation this summer?

   Susan: Chip (a) _____ start a new job in July, so we (b) _____ be able to go on vacation. We (c) _____ stay home and go to the beach.

3. **Eugene:** What's Jason going to major in at the university?

   Carol: Well, he really loves the ocean, so he (a) _____ major in marine biology, or he (b) _____ major in environmental science.

4. **Priscilla:** Will you go back to your country after you finish college here?

   Arnaldo: I don't know. I (a) _____ want to go back to visit my family, but I (b) _____ want to go back to live. There (c) _____ be more job opportunities for me here in the United States.

What are your plans for the future? Complete your chart with a base verb. Exchange charts with your partner. Report your partner's plans to the class.

EXAMPLE: He**'s going to, might, may, will go to** see a movie this evening.

	Base Verb	Will/Going to	May/Might
1. This evening,	to see a movie	X	
2. This weekend,			
3. Tomorrow night,			
4. A week from today,			
5. In 3 months,			
6. Next summer,			
7. In 5 years,			

What is our future in the computer age? Make statements with affirmative or negative forms of *will*, *be going to*, *may*, or *might*.

EXAMPLE: Computers/always be part of our lives

Computers will always be part of our lives.

1. People/want to go back to a time before computers
2. The number of computers in the world/increase
3. We/all have pocket computers
4. The Internet/connect people in every home all over the world
5. Students in classrooms all around the world/be able to "talk" to each other
6. People/learn languages easily with computers
7. People/prefer to communicate by computer
8. Books/disappear
9. People who cannot use computers/be able to find jobs
10. Computers/take away our privacy.

Activities

ACTIVITY 1

What do you think the world will be like in 2050? Think about changes in travel, the home, food, technology, and people, etc. With your group, write down ten changes. Discuss your group's ideas with the rest of the class.

ACTIVITY 2

Imagine that you and your partner win $1,000. You have one day to spend it. What are you going to do together? Give details of your activities. For example, if you rent a car, say what kind of car you are going to rent (a sports car, a limousine, a jeep?). Share your plans with the class. Decide which pair has the most interesting plans.

ACTIVITY 3

Make a weekly calendar and fill in your schedule for next week. Write different activities for each day. Try to make a date to do something with your partner in the future.

EXAMPLE: What are you going to do on Sunday?

I'm going to go jogging in Central Park.

ACTIVITY 4

You are a group of tourists going to Europe. You are at the airport and the tour guide is giving you some information.

 STEP ❶ Listen to the tour guide, and complete the travel plan below.

Day	Place	Number of Days/Nights
Sunday	Paris	
		3 nights
	Milan	
Saturday		
	Vienna	
Thursday		
Saturday		

STEP ❷ Compare your plan with a partner's.

STEP ❸ Tell the class your travel plans, real or imaginary. Say when you are going to go, how you are going to go there, where you are going to stay, etc.

>**EXAMPLE:** In June, I'm going to go to Vancouver alone. I'm going to fly there. I'm going to visit my uncle, who lives there.

ACTIVITY 5

STEP ❶ Sit in a circle with your whole class or a group of six to eight people. On the top of a blank piece of paper write:

On _____ in the year 2015, _____
      (today's date)   (your name)

STEP ❷ Pass the sheet of paper to the person on your left. This person writes a prediction about you for the year 2015. Then he or she passes the paper to the left for the next person to write a second prediction.

STEP ❸ Continue until everyone has written their predictions. At the end of the activity, you will have a list of predictions. Read the predictions and choose the best one. Read them aloud to the class.

Phrasal Verbs

Nervous Nellie Gives a Talk

Nelly is nervous about the talk she is going to give.

STEP ❶ Look at the pictures and describe the steps in Nellie's talk.

STEP ❷ Nelly has index cards to help her remember what to do. Read the first part of each index card. Find the second part of each card in the box, and read each complete card aloud.

sit down	calm down	take out
call up	ask for	stand up
put on		slow down

1.
Take a deep breath and _____ .

2.
_____ and introduce myself.

3.
_____ my glasses.

4.
_____ my notes.

5.
Don't talk too fast. _____ .

6.
_____ questions.

7.
_____ and relax.

8.
_____ all my friends and tell them it's over.

Phrasal Verbs

EXAMPLES	EXPLANATIONS
(a) Turn on the slide projector.	A phrasal verb is: a verb + a particle *turn* + *on* *sit* + *down* *stand* + *up*
(b) Plants grow. (grow = to increase in size) Children **grow up.** (grow up = to become an adult)	The verb + particle together have a specific meaning.

EXERCISE 1

Look at Nelly's index cards from the Opening Task on page 326 and circle all the phrasal verbs.

1. Take a deep breath and (calm down.)
2. Stand up and introduce myself.
3. Put on my glasses.
4. Take out my notes.
5. Turn out the lights.
6. Turn on the slide projector and show the slides.
7. Don't talk too fast. Slow down.
8. Turn off the slide projector.
9. Turn on the lights.
10. Ask for questions.
11. Sit down and relax.
12. Call up all my friends and tell them it's over!

Read each statement on the left to your partner. Your partner chooses a response from the right.

Statement

1. I don't want to cook tonight.
2. It's hot in here.
3. It's so quiet in here.
4. I can't read the map. The print's too small.
5. I can't do my homework with the TV on.
6. I'm bored.
7. My feet hurt.
8. I'm sleepy.
9. I'm really upset about our argument today.
10. I'm tired of sitting on this plane.

Response

a. Calm down.
b. Call up a friend.
c. Stand up for a few minutes.
d. Sit down for a while.

e. Lie down and take a nap.
f. Take off your jacket.

g. Put on your glasses.
h. Turn off the TV.
i. Let's eat out.

j. Turn on the radio.

 FOCUS 2 >>>>>>>>>>>>>>>>>> **MEANING/USE**

Phrasal Verbs

EXAMPLES	EXPLANATIONS
(a) I **hung up** the picture.	Sometimes the meaning of a phrasal verb is clear from the verb + particle combination.
(b) I **ran into** Joe on the street the other day.	Sometimes it is difficult to guess the meaning of a phrasal verb.
	The meaning of *ran into* is not the combination of *ran* and *into*. *Run into* means "to meet someone by chance."
	In informal English, phrasal verbs are more frequent than one-word verbs with the same meaning.
(c) Please **put out** your cigarette, Jake.	In (c), you are talking to a friend.
(d) Please **extinguish** your cigarettes, ladies and gentlemen.	In (d), a flight attendant is speaking to passengers on an airplane.

Circle the phrasal verbs. Then match each phrasal verb with a one-word verb.

**One-word verb
with same
meaning**

Sentences with phrasal verbs

1. I called 911 Emergency. The firefighters will be here soon to (put out) the fire.
2. Don't just stand at the door. Come in.
3. Fill out the application.
4. We're going to practice some phrasal verbs. Henry, can you please hand out this exercise?
5. I left my book at school. I don't remember the homework for tonight. I'll call up Manny and ask him.
6. I can't talk to you now. Come back in fifteen minutes.
7. I can't concentrate! Would you please turn down the music!
8. I am freezing in this house. Please turn up the heat.
9. Please take off your wet shoes.
10. Hold on a minute. I'm not ready yet.

raise

remove

telephone

extinguish

enter

distribute

complete

wait

lower

return

Fill in the blanks with the phrasal verbs below.

put away	turn on	pick up	throw away	turn off

DIRECTIONS FOR LANGUAGE LAB ASSISTANTS

When you leave the language lab, there are several things you must do. First, (1) _____ all the trash from the floor. Then (2) _____ all the equipment—tape recorders, VCRs, etc. (3) _____ all the cassettes students used. (4) _____ any coffee cups or trash students left in the room. Finally, (5) _____ the alarm system before you lock the doors.

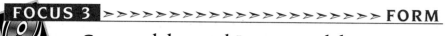

FOCUS 3

Separable and Inseparable Phrasal Verbs

Separable Phrasal Verbs

EXAMPLES				EXPLANATIONS
	Verb Particle			When the direct object is a noun, it can go:
(a) The teacher	**handed out**	the exercise.		• after the particle (*out*)
	Verb	**Direct Object**	**Particle**	
(b) The teacher	**handed**	the exercise	**out.**	• between the verb (*handed*) and the particle (*out*)
(c) The teacher handed **it** out. NOT: The teacher handed out **it**.				When the direct object is a pronoun, it always goes between the verb and the particle.

Inseparable Phrasal Verbs

EXAMPLES	EXPLANATIONS
(d) I **ran into** an old friend on the street. **(e)** I **ran into** her on the street. NOT: I **ran** an old friend **into** on the street. NOT: I **ran** her **into** on the street.	The direct object—noun or pronoun—goes after the particle.

Sergeant Strict is giving orders to his new soldiers. Repeat the Sergeant's orders in a different way each time.

1. (a) "Take off your civilian clothes."
   (b) "I *said,* take your civilian clothes off ."
   (c) "*Come on,* take them off !"

2. (a) "Hand out these uniforms."
   (b) "I said, _____."
   (c) "Come on, _____!"

3. (a) "Put on your new Army clothes."
   (b) "I said, _____."
   (c) "Come on, _____!"

4. (a) "Turn down that radio."
   (b) "I said, _____."
   (c) "Come on, _____!"

5. (a) "Put away your old clothes."
   (b) "I said, _____."
   (c) "Come on, _____!"

6. (a) "Throw out that junk food from home."
   (b) "I said, _____."
   (c) "Come on, _____!"

7. (a) "Clean up this mess."
   (b) "I said, _____."
   (c) "Come on, _____!"

8. (a) "Turn off the lights!"
   (b) "I said, _____."
   (c) "Come on, _____!"

Common Separable and Inseparable Phrasal Verbs

Separable Phrasal Verbs

SEPARABLE PHRASAL VERBS	MEANING	EXAMPLES
calm down	relax	**(a)** She is very upset about the accident. We can't **calm** her **down.**
call up	telephone	**(b)** I **called** my friend **up** the other night to ask about the homework.
cheer up	become happy, make someone happy	**(c)** My friend failed her final exam, so I brought her flowers to **cheer** her **up.**
clean up	clean	**(d)** **Clean** your room **up** before you watch TV!
figure out	solve, understand	**(e)** This puzzle is very confusing. I can't **figure** it **out.**
fill out	complete	**(f)** **Fill out** the application for a new license.
fill up	fill	**(g)** **Fill** it **up** with regular gas, please.
hand out	distribute	**(h)** The teacher **handed** the tests **out** to the the class.
hang up	place on a hanger or hook	**(i)** My husband never **hangs** his clothes **up**. **(j)** Please **hang up** the phone.
look up	search for in a reference book	**(k)** I didn't know his telephone number, so I **looked** it **up** in the phone book.

pick up	collect, lift	**(l)** In my neighborhood, they **pick up** the garbage every Tuesday.
		(m) I **picked** my pen **up** and started to write.
put away	put in its usual place	**(n)** My kids are neat! They always **put** their toys **away** .
put on	dress yourself	**(o)** It's really cold outside, so **put** a coat **on**.
put out	extinguish	**(p)** It took firefighters a few hours to **put** the fire **out**.
take off	remove	**(q)** **Take** your shoes **off** before you come into the house.
take out	put something outside	**(r)** Will you please **take** the garbage **out** ?
throw out/away	put in the garbage	**(s)** I have a lot of old things in the garage. I need to **throw** them **out.**
turn down	lower the volume	**(t)** It's 2:00 in the morning. **Turn** that stereo **down**!
turn off	stop the power	**(u)** There aren't any good programs on TV tonight. **Turn** it **off.**
turn on	start the power	**(v)** I always **turn on** the radio in the morning.
turn up	increase the volume	**(w)** When I hear my favorite song, I **turn** the volume **up**.
wake up	to open your eyes; to finish sleeping; to interrupt someone's sleep	**(x)** Be quiet! Don't **wake** the baby **up**.

Inseparable Phrasal Verbs

INSEPARABLE PHRASAL VERBS	MEANING	EXAMPLES
get in *get out of**	enter and leave a vehicle (car, taxi, truck)	**(y)** I **got in** my car and drove away. **(z)** My bag fell when I **got out of** the cab.
get on *get off*	enter and leave other forms of transportation (bus, plane, train)	**(aa)** I **got on** the train at 42nd Street. **(bb)** I **got off** the bus in front of the school.
go over	review	**(cc)** I **went over** my notes before the test.
run into	meet by chance	**(dd)** I **ran into** an old friend the other day.

*Sometimes phrasal verbs have three parts.

EXERCISE 6

Fill in the blanks with the phrasal verbs below. Use a pronoun in the second blank of each dialogue.

EXAMPLE: (clean up)

Mother: Danny, don't forget to (a) _clean up_ the mess in your bedroom.

Danny: Mom, I (b) _cleaned it up_ this morning.

pick up	cheer up	hand out	throw out	fill out

1. **Counselor:** You need to (a) _____ this application for college.

   Abdul: Can I (b) _____ at home?

2. **Susie:** Danny, I think it's time to (a) _____ all these old newspapers.

   Danny: I'm (b) _____ right now.

3. **Jackie:** Could you please (a) _____ that paper on the floor for me?

   Mark: I'll (b) _____ in a minute!

4. **Ms. Wagner:** Can you help me (a) _____ these exams, Wang?

   Wang: Sure, I'll (b) _____ right now.

5. **Mom:** Please try to (a) _____ your sister. She's in a bad mood.

   Bobbie: No one can (b) _____ . She's always in a bad mood.

EXERCISE 7

Sylvia is working late tonight. She's calling her husband, Abe, to see if he has done all the things on her list. Role-play the dialogue with a partner.

> **EXAMPLE: Sylvia:** Did you pick up the children at school?
>
> **Abe:** Yes, dear. I picked them up.

1. pick up your shirts at the cleaners
2. clean up the kitchen
3. put away the clean laundry
4. take out the dog
5. throw out the old flowers in the vase
6. fill up the car with gas
7. pick up a pizza for dinner
8. turn on the movie for the children
9. call up Warren to invite him to dinner

Common Phrasal Verbs without Objects

Some phrasal verbs do not take an object.

PHRASAL VERBS WITHOUT OBJECTS	MEANING	EXAMPLES
break down	stop working	**(a)** My car **broke down** last night.
come back	return	**(b)** He left home and never **came back.**
come in	enter	**(c) Come in** and make yourself comfortable.
eat out	eat in a restaurant	**(d)** I hate to cook, so I often **eat out.**
grow up	become an adult	**(e)** I **grew up** in the United States.
show up	appear	**(f)** After two hours, he finally **showed up.**
sit down	sit	**(g)** I feel tired, so I think I'll **sit down** for a while.
stand up	stand	**(h)** In some countries, students **stand up** when the teacher enters the room.

EXERCISE 8

Fill in the blanks with a phrasal verb from the box.

stand up	sit down	break down	eat out
show up	come in	come back	grow up

What do you say when . . . ?

1. you are very late for an important date:

   "Oh, I'm so sorry. Please forgive me, my car _____."

2. your friend's child runs away from home:

   "Don't worry, Elliot; I'm sure she'll _____ home very soon."

3. a teenager is sitting and an elderly man is standing on the bus:

   "_____ and give that man your seat."

4. your thirty-year-old friend is acting like a child:

   "Come on, Matt, _____ . You're not a child anymore."

5. you are a car salesperson and you are trying to get people into your showroom:

   "Please _____ , folks. We have many new models this year."

6. you and your roommate are hungry, but you're too tired to cook:

   "Let's _____ ."

7. your friend is crying about her date last night:

   Tammy: "What happened, Cheryl? Don't tell me your date didn't _____ last night?"

   Cheryl: "Oh, he did! That's why I'm crying!"

8. you are a receptionist in a very busy doctor's office and a patient is complaining about waiting so long:

   "Please _____ , Mr. Brody. The doctor will be with you in a few minutes."

Put the pictures in the correct order. Then fill in each blank with a phrasal verb from the box below.

_____

_____   _____

fill up	look up	break down
figure out	wake up	calm down
turn on	get out of	take out

It was a cold and rainy night. Forgetful Phil was on his way to visit his mother when his car suddenly (1) _____ . He was angry and upset, but after a while, he (2) _____ . It was dark, so Phil (3) _____ a flashlight. Then he took out his car manual. He tried to (4) _____ , *What to do when your car breaks down in the middle of nowhere*, but he didn't find anything in the manual. Next, he (5) _____ the car and looked under the hood. He wasn't able to (6) _____ the problem. Then Phil began to understand. He asked himself, "Did I (7) _____ my tank with gas?" Near the car there was a house. He knocked on the door and shouted, but nobody answered. There were no other houses. There was no telephone. "What now??" Phil thought. Then, just as he turned around to go back to his car, another car crashed into the back of his car. Suddenly, the people in the house (8) _____ and (9) _____ the lights. Phil sat down on the ground and began to cry!

Activities

Work with a partner to create a story or dialogue about the situation below. Role-play the situation for the class. The phrasal verbs in the box will help you.

Situation: It is 11:00 P.M. You are sleeping very deeply. Suddenly, you hear some loud noise coming from the apartment downstairs. Your neighbor's stereo is very loud.

wake up	throw out	turn down	turn off
turn on	go back	calm down	call up

ACTIVITY 2

Work in a group or as a whole class. The first person begins a story. He or she says, "I woke up . . ." and completes the sentence. The second person repeats the first sentence and adds a second sentence using a phrasal verb. The third person repeats the first two sentences and then adds a third, and so on. Don't write anything down. Use your memory! Refer to the phrasal verbs from this unit.

EXAMPLE: **Player #1:** I woke up early.

Player #2: I woke up early, and turned off the alarm clock.

Player #3: I woke up early, turned off the alarm clock, and took off my pajamas.

ACTIVITY 3

STEP ❶ Work in a group. Put numbers 1 to 12 in a bag. Pick out a number from the bag. Read the sentence in the box that corresponds to your number and then do the action.

STEP ❷ After the group has done all the actions, write sentences about the things you did.

EXAMPLE: Mario put on Marcela's cap.

José turned off the light.

1. Put on a piece of a classmate's clothing or jewelry.	2. Turn off the light.	3. You spill a cup of hot coffee on yourself and on the floor. Clean it up.
4. Call up a friend and tell him or her you are sick.	5. Draw a picture of yourself on a piece of paper and hang it up on the wall.	6. Stand up. Put your hands on your head. Then sit down.
7. Cheer a classmate up.	8. Hand your telephone number out to all the people in the group.	9. Take something out of your pocket and throw it away.
10. Take off an article of clothing and put it on someone else.	11. Turn on something electrical (tape recorder, radio, light, etc.) and then turn it off.	12. Pretend you find a word whose meaning you don't know. Look it up in the dictionary.

ACTIVITY 4

Amy wants to buy a jacket. She goes to a store.

 STEP ❶ Listen to the conversation. Then look at the statements below. Check True or False.

	True	False
1. The store doesn't have any size ten jackets.	_____	_____
2. The jacket Amy tries on fits perfectly.	_____	_____
3. Amy thinks the jacket is too expensive.	_____	_____
4. Amy doesn't like the pink jacket she is wearing.	_____	_____
5. Amy will return to the store.	_____	_____

STEP ❷ Listen to the conversation again and complete the phrasal verbs you hear below:

take _____   put _____   throw _____   come _____   come _____

STEP ❸ Compare the phrasal verbs you found with those your partner found. Now make a dialogue on a similar topic with your partner. Use the five phrasal verbs in the dialogue and others from this unit.

STEP ❹ Role-play your dialogue in front of the class.

UNIT

22

Comparison with Adjectives

Comparison Shopping for an Apartment

You are a college student and are looking for an apartment. You study during the day and have a part-time job at night.

FOR RENT
Studio Apartment. 200 square feet. Close to bus stop and market. Fully furnished. $500/month plus utilities.

FOR RENT
One-bedroom apartment. 900 square feet. Quiet. Lots of light. $800/month including utilities.

STEP ❶ Look at the apartment ads. Read the statements below about the studio apartment. Check ( ) Yes, No, or Maybe.

			YES	NO	MAYBE
The studio apartment is	1. smaller	than the one bedroom apartment			
	2. closer to the subway				
	3. farther away from the downtown area				
	4. more expensive				
	5. more spacious				
	6. noisier				
	7. safer				
	8. more convenient				
	9. sunnier				
	10. quieter				

STEP ❷ Which apartment is better? Give reasons for your choice.

I think the _____ is better because . . .

Comparative Form of Adjectives

Regular Comparatives

There are two regular comparative forms of adjectives in English.

1. For adjectives with one syllable or those ending in *-y*:

   X *is* _____ *er than* Y.

EXAMPLE	ADJECTIVE	COMPARATIVE	RULE
(a) This neighborhood is **safer than** that one.	*safe*	*safer than*	For adjectives ending in *-e*, add *-r*.
(b) The one-bedroom apartment is **bigger than** the studio.	*big*	*bigger than*	For adjectives that end in consonant-vowel-consonant, double the consonant, add *-er*.
(c) The studio is **noisier than** the one bedroom.	*noisy*	*noisier than*	For adjectives ending in *-y*, change the *-y* to *i*, add *-er*.
(d) The studio is **smaller than** the one-bedroom.	*small*	*smaller than*	For all other adjectives, add *-er*.

2. For adjectives with two or more syllables:

   X *is* (*more/less*) _____ *than* Y.

EXAMPLE	ADJECTIVE	COMPARATIVE	RULE
(e) The studio is **more economical than** the one-bedroom.	*economical*	*more economical than*	Use *more* or *less* before the adjective
(f) The studio is **less expensive than** the one-bedroom.	*expensive*	*less expensive than*	

NOTES:

- Some adjectives with two syllables can take either *-er* or *more/less*. For example: *quiet— quieter* or *more quiet*.
- In formal English we say: Joe is taller than **I** (am).
  In informal English we sometimes say: Joe is taller than **me.**

Irregular Comparatives

EXAMPLES	EXPLANATIONS
(g) This neighborhood is **better than** that one. **(h)** This year's winter was **worse than** last year's (winter). **(i)** The one-bedroom is **farther** away from the bus stop **than** the studio is.	The comparative forms of *good, bad,* and *far* are irregular. *good—better* *bad—worse* *far—farther*
(j) This apartment is **much better than** that one. **(k)** This apartment is **much larger than** the other one.	Use *much* to make a comparison stronger.

EXERCISE 1

Write the comparative form of each adjective + *than* in parentheses.

EXAMPLE: A cat is (big) _bigger than_____ a mouse.

1. a. A tiger is (large) _____ a cat.

   b. It is (dangerous) _____ a cat.

2. a. Outgoing people are (nervous) _____ shy people.

   b. They are (comfortable) _____ in social situations.

3. a. The weather in Spain is (hot) _____ the weather in Sweden.

   b. The food in hot countries is (spicy) _____ the food in cold countries.

4. a. Dog lovers say cats are (intelligent) _____ dogs.

   b. Cat lovers think cats are (good) _____ dogs.

5. Today wasn't a very good day.

   a. We hope tomorrow will be (good) _____ today.

   b. We hope it will be (exciting) _____ today.

Fill in the blanks with the comparative form of the adjective.

Jane: Kevin, I found these two apartment ads in the newspaper this morning. There's a studio and a one-bedroom. I think the one-bedroom sounds nice. What do you think?

Kevin: Well, the one-bedroom is definitely (1) (large) _____ than the studio, but the studio is (2) (cheap) _____. You know you only have a part-time job. How can you afford to pay $750 a month for rent?

Jane: I know the one-bedroom is (3) expensive _____, but I have so much furniture. The one-bedroom is (4) (big) _____ and I want to have guests visit and it will be much (5) (comfortable) _____. Besides, maybe someday I'll have a roommate, and I'll need a (6) (spacious) _____ apartment, Kevin. Right?

Kevin: Well, maybe, but you need to be realistic. The studio is in the center of town. You'll be (7) (close) _____ to transportation, stores, the library, and the college.

Jane: You're much (8) (practical) _____ than I am, Kevin. But the studio is directly over a video store, so it will be (9) (noisy) _____ than the one-bedroom. I will need peace and quiet so I can study.

Kevin: Listen—the studio is small, but it's much (10) (cozy) _____ than the one-bedroom and you'll spend much less time cleaning it!

Jane: True, but I think the one-bedroom will be much (11) (safe) _____ and (12) (good) _____ for me than the studio.

Kevin: It seems to me your mind is made up.

Jane: Yes, it is. By the way, Kevin, I'm going to see the one-bedroom later today. Can you come with me?

Kevin: Sure.

Write an advertisement for each product on the left. Compare it to the product on the right. Use the adjectives below.

EXAMPLE: _"Double Chocolate" cake tastes richer than "Chocolate Surprise."_

1. **Product:** Double Chocolate Cake Mix

   Compare with Chocolate Surprise Cake Mix.

   Adjectives: rich, creamy, delicious, sweet, thick, fattening

_____

_____

_____

2. **Product:** Genie Laundry Detergent

   Compare with Bubbles Laundry Detergent

   Adjectives: strong, effective, expensive, fast-acting, gentle

_____

_____

_____

3. **Product:** Save-a-Watt Space Heater

   Compare with Consumer Space Heater

   Adjectives: efficient, safe, reliable, small, economical, practical

_____

_____

_____

Yoko wants to study English in the United States. She knows about an English program in Brattleboro, a small town in Vermont. She also knows about a program in Los Angeles, a big city in California. She needs to decide where she wants to live. Here is some information about the two places.

	Brattleboro, Vermont	**Los Angeles, California**
1. Rent for a one-bed apt.	$450 a month	$1,000 a month
2. Population	12,000	3 million
3. Weather	cold in winter	warm in winter
	hot in summer	hot in summer
4. Public Transportation	not good	good
5. Quality of Life		
a. the environment	clean	not so clean
b. the crime rate	low	high
c. lifestyle	relaxed	busy
d. the streets	quiet	noisy

Make comparative statements about Brattleboro and Los Angeles.

1. crime rate (low/high) _The crime rate is lower in Brattleboro than in Los Angeles._

2. (populated) _____

3. (cheap/expensive) _____

4. public transportation (good/bad) _____

5. winters (cold) _____

6. (dangerous/safe) _____

7. (clean/dirty) _____

8. (quiet/noisy) _____

9. (relaxed/busy) _____

10. In your opinion, which place is better for Yoko? Why?

_____

_____

FOCUS 2 >>>>>>>>>>>>>>>>>>>>>>>> FORM

Questions with Comparative Adjectives

EXAMPLES

(a) Is the one-bedroom **more expensive than** the studio?

(b) Are studios **better than** apartments?

(c) Are studios **less practical than** one bedroom apartments?

(d) **Who** is **older,** you or your brother?

(e) **Which** is **more difficult,** English or Chinese?

(f) **Whose** apartment is **more comfortable,** yours or hers?

EXERCISE 5

Go back to the Opening Task on page 342 and ask a partner *yes/no* questions about the studio and the one-bedroom apartment.

EXAMPLE: economical

Is the studio more economical than the one-bedroom?

Yes, it is.

1. practical
2. far from the downtown area
3. small
4. cheap
5. sunny
6. comfortable
7. economical

8. roomy
9. quiet
10. convenient
11. close to the subway
12. pretty
13. large
14. good

EXERCISE 6

Interview your partner. Answer each other's questions.

EXAMPLE: Question: Is a theater ticket more expensive than a movie ticket?

Answer: Yes, it is. No, it isn't. OR I'm not sure.

1. people in the United States/friendly/people in other countries
2. English grammar/difficult/the grammar of your native language
3. a house/good/an apartment
4. a single person's life/exciting/a married person's life
5. reading/interesting/watching TV
6. electric heat/economical/gas heat
7. men/romantic/women
8. a Japanese watch/expensive/a Swiss watch
9. The American population/diverse/the population in your native country

EXERCISE 7

Ask a partner questions with *who*, *which*, or *whose* and the words in parentheses. Answer each other's questions.

EXAMPLE: (popular) Who is more popular, Madonna or Tina Turner?

(practical) Which is less practical, a cordless phone or a regular phone?

1. (intelligent) women or men?
2. (difficult) speaking English or writing English?
3. (hard) a man's work or a woman's work?
4. (bad) ironing or vacuuming?
5. (cheap) a public college or a private college?
6. (interesting) a taxi cab driver's job or a scientist's job?
7. (powerful) a four-cylinder car or a five-cylinder car?
8. (dangerous) a motorcycle or a car?
9. (sensitive) a man or a woman?
10. (good) Madonna's voice or Tina Turner's voice?
11. (delicious) Chinese food or Italian food?
12. (spicy) Indian food or Japanese food?
13. (American) jazz or salsa music?

FOCUS 3 >>>>>>>>>>>>>>>>>>>>>> **MEANING**

Expressing Similarities and Differences with As . . . As

EXAMPLES	EXPLANATIONS
(a) Mark is **as tall as** Sam. **(b)** Tokyo is **as crowded as** Hong Kong.	To say two things are equal or the same, use *as* + adjective + *as*.
(c) Mark is**n't as tall as** Steve. (= Steve is taller than Mark.) **(d)** The studio is**n't as expensive as** the one-bedroom.	To say there is a difference between two things, use *not as* + adjective + *as*.

EXERCISE 8

Here is a dialogue between Tommy and his mother. Write the correct form of the comparative in the blanks. Use *-er*, *more than*, *less than*, and *as . . . as*.

Mother: Tommy, I don't want you to buy a motorcycle. Why don't you buy a car instead? A car is (1) _more convenient than_ (convenient) a motorcycle and it's (2) _____ (practical), too.

Tommy: Maybe it's more practical, but a car isn't (3) _____ (economical) a motorcycle. I can get fifty miles to a gallon with a motorcycle! And a motorcycle's (4) _____ (cheap) a car.

Mother: Listen to me. You live in a big city. There are a lot of crazy people out there on the streets. A car is (5) _____ (safe) a motorcycle.

Tommy: Mom, I'm a good driver. I'm (6) _____ (good) you are. Besides that, it's (7) _____ (easy) to park a motorcycle in the city than it is to park a car.

Mother: Well, you're right about that. But I'm still your mother and you live in my house, so you will do as I say! When you are (8) _____ (old), you can do whatever you want.

Tommy: But all my friends are getting motorcycles, Mom. I won't look (9) _____ (cool) my friends.

Mother: I don't care, Tommy. Maybe their mothers aren't (10) _____ (nervous) I am, or (11) _____ (concerned) I am. My answer is no and that's final.

EXERCISE 9

Work with a partner and make *yes/no* questions with *as . . . as* about the countries you are from with the words below.

EXAMPLE: capital city/big

  Is Quito as big as Santiago?

1. capital city/big
2. foreign cars in . . . /expensive
3. the school year in . . . /long
4. soccer in . . . /popular
5. your hometown/safe

6. teenagers in your country/ interested in rock music
7. beaches/crowded
8. foreign films/popular

FOCUS 4 ➤➤➤➤➤➤➤➤➤➤➤➤➤➤➤➤➤➤➤➤➤➤ **USE**

Making Polite Comparisons

EXAMPLES	EXPLANATIONS
(a) Hamid is **shorter than** Marco. **(b)** Hamid is **not as tall as** Marco.	Sentence (b) is more polite. To make a polite comparison, use *not as* + adjective + *as*.

EXERCISE 10

You are "Blunt Betty." Read a statement from Column A. Your statements are very direct and a little impolite. Your partner, "Polite Polly," makes a statement with *not as* + adjective + *as* to make your statement more polite.

Column A

Blunt Betty

Column B

Polite Polly

1. Marco is fatter than Jonathan.

    (thin)

    Marco is not as thin as Jonathan.

2. London is dirtier than Paris.   (clean)
3. Science class is more boring than math.   (interesting)
4. Your child is lazier than mine.   (energetic)
5. Your car is slower than ours.   (fast)
6. Detroit is more dangerous than Boston.   (safe)
7. This book is worse than that book.   (good)
8. Your apartment is smaller than ours.   (big)
9. Miguel's pronunciation is worse than Maria's.   (good)
10. American coffee is weaker than Turkish coffee.   (strong)
11. Your salary is lower than mine.   (high)

EXERCISE 11

Use the categories below to write statements comparing yourself to a partner. Then report your information to the class.

EXAMPLE: My partner's older than I am. My partner's older than me.

I'm not as old as he is. I'm not as old as him.

	Me	**My Partner**
1. Age	19	24
2. Height		
3. Hair length		
4. Hair color		
5. Personality		
6. Other		

Correct the errors in the following sentences.

1. John is more tall than Mary.

2. Seoul is more safer than Los Angeles.

3. Paul is as intelligent than Robert.

4. Mary is not beautiful as Kim.

5. My test scores were more worse than Margaret's.

6. Lorraine's eyes are darker than me.

7. Jeff is more handsomer than Jack.

8. My parent's life was hard than mine.

9. Is New York exciting as Paris?

10. Is Lake Ontario cleaner that Lake Erie?

11. The Hudson River is polluted as the Volga River.

12. Mexico's capital city is more crowded than the United States.

Activities

How much do the following things cost in your country? Write the cost in United States dollars for each thing in your country. Ask a classmate the prices of the same things in his or her country. Add three items of your own. Present your comparisons to the class.

EXAMPLE: A gallon of gas is more expensive in Italy than in Mexico.

	Your Country	Your Classmate's Country
1. a gallon of gas		
2. a movie ticket		
3. bus fare		
4. a pair of jeans		
5. a cup of coffee		
6. rent for a one-bedroom apartment		
7. a newspaper		
8.		
9.		
10.		

ACTIVITY 2

Work in a group. Write six statements comparing cities, countries, or other places in the world. Make three statements that are true and three statements that are false. Read the statements to the class. The class guesses if they are true or false.

EXAMPLE: The United States is larger than the People's Republic of China. (False)

The Pacific Ocean is bigger than the Atlantic Ocean. (True)

ACTIVITY 3

STEP ❶ Look at the list of adjectives. Check *Very*, *Average*, or *Not Very* for each.

STEP ❷ Compare with a partner. Write a comparative sentence for each adjective.

STEP ❸ Then, tell the class about you and your partner.

    EXAMPLE: I'm more talkative than my partner.

               He's less practical than I am.

               I'm as moody as he is.

	Very	*Average*	*Not Very*
1. talkative	_____	_____	_____
2. friendly	_____	_____	_____
3. shy	_____	_____	_____
4. neat	_____	_____	_____
5. practical	_____	_____	_____
6. optimistic	_____	_____	_____
7. moody	_____	_____	_____
8. lazy	_____	_____	_____
9. funny	_____	_____	_____
10. athletic	_____	_____	_____
11. jealous	_____	_____	_____
12. serious	_____	_____	_____
13. _____	_____	_____	_____
14. _____	_____	_____	_____
15. _____	_____	_____	_____

ACTIVITY 4

Work with a partner. Find a product or service you want to sell. Find a name for it. Then write a thirty-second radio commercial for the product or service. Present your commercials to the class.

ACTIVITY 5

STEP ❶ Compare life today with life fifty years ago. Read the first four sentences on the chart on the next page and then add six sentences of your own. Check Agree or Disagree under You. Then ask your partner and check Agree or Disagree.

	You		Your Partner	
	Agree	Disagree	Agree	Disagree
1. Life is more difficult.				
2. People are happier.				
3. Families are stronger.				
4. Children are more intelligent.				
5.				
6.				
7.				
8.				
9.				
10.				

STEP ❷ Compare your answers with your partner's. Then write six sentences that compare life today with life fifty years ago.

EXAMPLE: Today, children are more intelligent. They are more independent.

ACTIVITY 6

STEP ❶ Look at the three different apartment ads. Listen and say which apartment, A, B, or C, each person is talking about.

FOR RENT: Studio apartment. 200 square feet.
Close to bus stop and supermarket.
Fully furnished. $500/month plus utilities.

FOR RENT: One-bedroom apartment. 900 square feet.
Quiet. Lots of light. $800/month including utilities.

FOR RENT: Two-bedroom apartment. 1,500 square feet.
Close to subway. Quiet area. $1,000/month plus utilities.

STEP ❷ Which apartment is it? Work in a group. Each person gives two facts about one of the apartments and the others guess which apartment it is.

EXAMPLE: It's more expensive than the studio. It's closer to the subway.

Is it the _____?

Yes, it is. No, it isn't.

23 Comparison with Adverbs

Comparing Men and Women

Check *Yes, No,* or *Maybe* for each question. Then talk about your answers with your classmates.

	Yes	No	Maybe
1. Do women work harder than men?			
2. Do men drive more safely than women?			
3. Do women communicate better than men?			
4. Do men dance more gracefully than women?			
5. Do women take care of children more patiently than men?			
6. Do men express their feelings more openly than women?			
7. Do women learn math more easily than men?			
8. Do men spend money more freely than women?			
9. Do women learn languages more easily than men?			
10. Do men think more clearly in emergencies than women?			

Comparative Forms of Adverbs

EXAMPLE	ADVERB/COMPARATIVE		RULE
(a) Women live **longer than** men.	*long*	*longer than*	For short adverbs, add *-er* + *than*.
(b) Do women drive **more safely than** men?	*safely*	*more/less safely than*	For adverbs with two or more syllables, use *more/less* + adverb + *than*.
(c) Do men drive **less carefully than** women?	*carefully*	*carefully than*	
(d) Eugene and Carol eat out much **more often than** Warren and Harriet.	*often*	*more/less often than*	With adverbs of frequency, use *more/less* + adverb + *than*.
(e) Do women cook **better than** men?	*well*	*better than*	With irregular adverbs, use the irregular form + *than*.
(f) Do boys do **worse** in school than girls?	*badly*	*worse than*	
(g) Can a man throw a ball **farther than** a woman?	*far*	*farther than*	

EXAMPLES	EXPLANATIONS
(h) Jason can climb higher than his brother (**can**). **(i)** She's better in school than I (**am**).	Sometimes, the auxiliary verb, for example *can*, *be*, or *will*, follows the subject after *than*.
(j) I type faster than my friend (**does**). **(k)** We speak Spanish better than they (**do**).	If there is no *be* or auxiliary verb, you can use *do*.
(l) I type faster than she (**does**). **(m)** I type faster than **her**.	In formal English, the subject pronoun follows *than*. In informal English, the object pronoun (*me, you, him, her, us, them*) follows *than*.

Go back to the questions in the Opening Task on page 358 and underline the comparatives with adverbs.

EXAMPLE: Do women live <u>longer than</u> men?

Write sentences comparing yourself with your partner. Use the verbs and adverbs in the chart.

Verb	Adverb	Comparisons
1. cry	easily	My partner cries more easily than I.
2. drive	carefully	
3. speak English	fluently	
4. exercise	regularly	
5. travel	often	
6. study	hard	
7. laugh	loudly	
8. participate in class	actively	
9. take exams	calmly	
10. read	fast	

FOCUS 2 >>>>>>>>>>>>>>>> FORM/MEANING

Expressing Similarities and Differences

EXAMPLES	EXPLANATIONS
(a) A woman can work **as hard as** a man. **(b)** A man can dance **as gracefully as** a woman.	To show similarities, use *as* + adverb + *as*.
(c) He does**n't** speak **as clearly as** I (do). **(d)** = I speak more clearly than he (does). **(e)** = He speaks less clearly than I (do).	To show differences, use *not as* + adverb + *as*.

EXERCISE 3

Sally Miller and Bill Benson are applying for a job as director of an art company. Decide who is better for the job. Make comparative statements about each person.

EXAMPLE: Sally works as hard as Bill.

Bill draws better than Sally./Sally doesn't draw as well as Bill.

Work Habits	Sally Miller	Bill Benson
1. works hard	X	X
2. draws well		X
3. thinks creatively	X	X
4. communicates openly	X	
5. plans carefully		X
6. works well with others	X	X
7. acts calmly in emergencies	X	
8. solves problems fairly		X
9. writes clearly	X	X
10. works fast		X

Imagine you are the president of the art company. You want to compare Sally and Bill. Write some questions to ask about them.

EXAMPLE: Does Sally work as hard as Bill?

Does Bill draw better than Sally?

For each statement you read, your partner says how he or she is similar or different.

EXAMPLE: You say: I (can) cook well.

Your partner says: I can cook as well as you.

I can't cook as well as you.

I can cook better than you.

1. speak clearly
2. dance gracefully
3. sing sweetly
4. jump high
5. run far
6. add numbers quickly
7. meet new people easily
8. tell a joke well
9. study hard
10. learn English fast

Discuss these questions before you read.

1. Do you think boys and girls grow up differently?
   In what ways do they grow up differently?
2. Do you think boys and girls talk to each other differently?
3. In what ways do you think boys and girls play differently?

Now, read the following:

Boys and girls grow up in different worlds. Research studies show that boys and girls act very differently. For example, when boys and girls play, they don't play together. Some of their activities are similar, but their favorite games are different. Also, the language they use in games is different.

Boys usually play outside in large groups. The group has a leader. The leader gives orders. There are winners and losers in boys' games. Boys frequently brag about how good they are at something and argue about who is the best.

Girls, on the other hand, play in small groups or pairs. The most important thing for a girl is her best friend. Closeness is very important to girls. Girls like to sit together and talk. In their games, like jump rope, everyone gets a turn. In many of their activities, such as playing together with their dolls, there are no winners or losers. Girls don't brag about how good they are at something. They don't give orders. They usually make suggestions.

Does this text say the same things you said in your discussion? What information is the same? What information is different?

EXERCISE 7

With the information from the reading, check True or False for the statements below.

	True	False
1. Boys and girls play differently.		
2. Boys and girls usually play with each other.		
3. Girls act more aggressively than boys.		
4. Girls play more competitively than boys do.		
5. Boys brag about how good they are at something more frequently than girls.		
6. Girls talk to each other more intimately than boys do.		
7. Girls give suggestions more frequently than boys.		
8. Boys play more cooperatively than girls do.		

Write statements to compare boys and girls. Use *more/less/as . . . as*. Discuss your answers with the class.

1. build things creatively

   Boys build things more creatively than girls.

   Girls build things as creatively as boys (do).

2. score high on math tests

3. run fast

4. act aggressively

5. act independently

6. learn languages easily

7. solve problems peacefully

8. make friends quickly

9. study hard

10. express feelings openly

FOCUS 3 ➤➤➤➤➤➤➤➤➤➤➤➤➤ **FORM/MEANING**

Questions with *How*

EXAMPLES	EXPLANATIONS
(a) **How old** are you? **(b)** **How well** do you speak English?	An adjective (*old, tall*) or an adverb (*well, far*) is often used in a *how* question.
(c) **How far** is it from here to the park? It's about five blocks.	*How far* asks about distance.
(d) **How long does it take** to fly from New York to Beijing? It takes about twenty-four hours. **(e)** **How long does it take** you to prepare dinner? It takes me an hour.	*How long does it take* asks about time.

Ask a partner questions with *how*. Fill in your partner's answers on the right. Your partner asks you the same questions, and fills in your answers on the left.

EXAMPLE: 1. How far do you live from school?

2. How well can you cook?

	You	Your Partner
1. how far/live from school	5 miles	4 blocks
2. how well/cook	very well	very well
3. how fast/fall asleep at night		
4. how far/run		
5. how hard/study		
6. how fast/type		
7. how late/stay up at night		
8. how early/get up in the morning		
9. how well/know your classmates		
10. how often/speak to your best friend		

Compare yourself with your partner for each of the questions in Exercise 9.

1. I live farther away from school than my partner (does). _____

2. My partner cooks as well as I (do). _____

3. _____

4. _____

5. _____

6. _____

7. _____

8. _____

9. _____

10. _____

Fill in the chart. Say how much time it takes you to do each of the activities below. Then interview a partner. Write statements with the comparative form of adverbs.

EXAMPLE: It takes me longer to do my homework.

	You	Your Partner
1. do your homework	1 hour	45 minutes
2. get dressed in the morning		
3. get to school		
4. clean your room/apartment/house		
5. have breakfast		
6. take a shower		
7. cook dinner		
8. fall asleep at night		

Activities

Write sentences comparing two cities or places that you know.

EXAMPLE: The trains run more smoothly in Berlin than in New York.

1. trains/run smoothly

2. buses/run efficiently

3. people/work hard

4. taxi drivers/drive carelessly

5. traffic/move slowly

6. people/talk quickly

7. people/talk to foreigners politely

8. stores/stay open late

9. people/drive fast

10. families/take vacations frequently

Add two sentences of your own:

11. _____

12. _____

ACTIVITY 2

STEP ❶ Here is a list of adverbs and a list of actions. Write each adverb and each action on a card.

Adverbs	Actions
Slowly	Eat spaghetti
Sadly	Put on your clothes
Nervously	Make the bed
Angrily	Cook dinner
Fast	Type a letter
Carefully	Brush your teeth
Seriously	Comb your hair
Happily	Paint a picture
Loudly	Play tennis
Enthusiastically	Shake someone's hand
Shyly	Look at someone

STEP ❷ Mix up each group of cards separately. With a partner, take one adverb card and one action card.

STEP ❸ Both of you mime the same action and adverb. The class guesses the action and the adverb.

STEP ❹ The class compares your two performances.

    EXAMPLE: Angrily/Eat spaghetti

        Paola ate spaghetti more angrily than Maria.

Planning a Vacation

Here is a map of the southwestern United States. You and your friend want to take a three-week vacation to visit the national parks. Start from Denver, Colorado, and list the places you will visit in order. Then fill in the chart on the next page. Ask questions with *how far* and *how long does it take* to decide on the route you will take and the time you will need. Remember you will travel by car and the average speed is sixty-five miles per hour.

EXAMPLE: How far is it from Denver to the Grand Canyon?

It's 780 miles.

How long does it take to get from Denver to the Grand Canyon?

It takes about twelve hours by car.

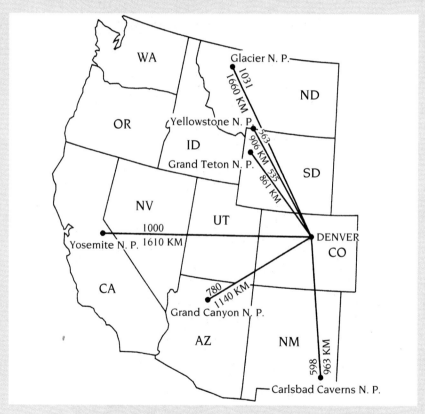

Depart from:	Denver, Colorado	Distance in miles/kilometers	Time
Stop 1			
2			
3			
4			
5			

ACTIVITY 4

Compare yourself with someone you know—a family member, a friend, your boyfriend/girlfriend, etc. Write ten sentences.

EXAMPLE: I dance better than my sister (does).

I can make friends more easily than she (does).

ACTIVITY 5

What does Richard like about London, England?

 STEP ❶ Listen to the tape and look at the list below. Check the things he thinks are good.

Richard likes . . .

1. _____ the people

2. _____ the hotel

3. _____ the buses

4. _____ the taxi drivers

5. _____ the subway

6. _____ English cooking

7. _____ the restaurants

STEP ❷ Listen again and say why Richard likes or dislikes the things.

STEP ❸ Tell the class about a place you visited. Use adverbs of comparison as much as possible.

24

Superlatives

General Knowledge Quiz

STEP ❶ Check the correct answer. Then compare your answers with your classmates'.

1. What is the largest ocean?
   a. Pacific   b. Atlantic   c. Indian

2. What's the most valuable painting in the world?
   a. Van Gogh's "Sunflowers"
   b. Leonardo da Vinci's "Mona Lisa"
   c. Rembrandt's "Self Portrait"

3. What's the most widely spoken language in the world?
   a. English   b. Spanish   c. Chinese

4. What's the hottest place in the world?
   a. Libya   b. Israel   c. Ethiopia

5. What's the tallest office building in the world?
   a. the Sears Tower, Chicago
   b. the World Trade Center, New York
   c. the Petronas Tower, Kuala Lumpur

6. What's the most crowded city in the world?
   a. Shanghai   b. Mexico City   c. Tokyo

7. What's the most expensive university in the United States?
   a. Harvard   b. Yale   c. M.I.T.

8. What's the wettest place in the world?
   a. Hawaii   b. India   c. Jamaica

9. What's the most nutritious fruit?
   a. banana   b. avocado   c. orange

10. What's the hardest gem?
    a. ruby   b. diamond   c. emerald

STEP ❷ Now write similar questions. Quiz your classmates.

11. _____

12. _____

13. _____

14. _____

15. _____

FOCUS 1 > MEANING

Superlatives

EXAMPLES	EXPLANATIONS
(a) **The tallest** building in the world is the Petronas Tower. **(b)** **The least expensive** food on the menu is a hamburger. **(c)** Rosa writes **the most carefully** of all.	Superlatives compare one thing or person to all the others in a group.
(d) Dr. Diaz is the most respected teacher **at the school.** **(e)** M.I.T. is the most expensive university **in the United States.** **(f)** Etsuko performs the best **of all the dancers.**	Use prepositional phrases after superlatives to identify the group.

EXERCISE 1

Go back to the Opening Task on page 372. Underline all the superlative forms in the questions.

EXAMPLE: What is the <u>largest</u> ocean?

Regular and Irregular Superlative Forms

Regular Forms

EXAMPLES	ADJECTIVE/ ADVERB	SUPERLATIVE FORM	RULE
(a) The Sears Tower in Chicago is **the tallest** building in the United States.	*tall*	*the tallest*	One-syllable adjectives or adverbs: *the* + adjective/adverb + *-est*.
(b) My grandfather worked **the hardest** of his three brothers.	*hard*	*the hardest*	
(c) Jupiter is **the largest** planet.	*large*	*the largest*	Adjectives/ Adverbs ending in *-e*: add *-st*.
(d) I get up **the latest** in my family.	*late*	*the latest*	
(e) The hottest place in the world is Ethiopia.	*hot*	*the hottest*	One-syllable adjectives, ending in consonant-vowel-consonant: double the final consonant, add *-est*.
(f) The easiest subject for me is geography.	*easy*	*the easiest*	Two-syllable adjectives/adverbs ending in *-y*: change *-y* to *-i*: add *-est*.
(g) She arrived **the earliest.**	*early*	*the earliest*	
(h) The most nutritious fruit is the avocado.	*nutritious*	*the most nutritious*	Adjectives/ adverbs with two or more syllables: use *the* + *most/ least*.
(i) The least expensive food on the menu is a hamburger.	*expensive*	*the least expensive*	
(j) Of all his friends, he drives **the most carefully.**	*carefully*	*the most carefully*	
(k) She danced **the least gracefully** of all the students.	*gracefully*	*the least gracefully*	

Irregular Forms

EXAMPLES	ADJECTIVE	ADVERB	SUPERLATIVE
(l) That college has **the best** professors.	good	well	the best
(m) That was **the worst** movie I saw last year.	bad	badly	the worst
(n) He ran is **the farthest.**	far	far	the farthest

EXERCISE 2

Here are some interesting facts from the *Guinness Book of World Records*. Write the superlative form of the adjective/adverb in parentheses in the blanks.

EXAMPLE: (cold) Antarctica is ___the coldest___ place on earth.

1. _____ (large) cucumber weighed sixty-six pounds.

2. _____ (popular) tourist attraction in the United States is Disney-world in Florida.

3. _____ (successful) pop group of all time is the Beatles.

4. _____ (heavy) baby at birth was a boy of twenty-two pounds eight ounces. He was born in Italy in 1955.

5. _____ (fat) person was a man in New York City. He weighed almost 1,200 pounds.

6. _____ (prolific) painter was Pablo Picasso. He produced about 13,500 paintings; 100,00 prints; 34,000 book illustrations; and 300 sculptures.

7. _____ (long) attack of hiccups lasted sixty-seven years.

8. _____ (big) omelet was made of 54,763 eggs with 531 pounds of cheese in Las Vegas, Nevada in 1986.

9. _____ (hot) city in the United States is Key West, Florida.

10. Mexico City is now the world's _____ (fast) growing city.

Fill in the name of a student in your class and the superlative form of each adverb.

Name   **Superlative**

1. _Juan_____ does the homework the   _most carefully_____ (carefully).

2. _____ speaks English   _____ (fluently).

3. _____ arrives in class   _____ (early).

4. _____ guesses new words   _____ (fast).

5. _____ raises his/her hand   _____ (often).

6. _____ understands English   _____ (well).

7. _____ communicates in English   _____ (effectively).

8. _____ participates in class   _____ (actively).

Add two statements of your own.

9. _____

10. _____

Information Gap. Work with a partner. One person looks at chart A, and the other person looks at Chart B on page E-5. Ask your partner questions to find out the missing information in your chart. Write the answers in the chart.

   EXAMPLE: **Student A:** What is the longest river in North America?

   Student B: The Mississippi.

CHART A

	North America	Central and South America	Asia	Europe	Africa	The World
long river		The Amazon		The Volga		The Nile
large country	Canada		The People's Republic of China		Sudan	
populated country		Brazil		Germany		The People's Republic of China
high mountain	Mt. McKinley		Mt. Everest		Mt. Kilimanjaro	
small country		Grenada		Vatican City		Vatican City

Play this Jeopardy game in two teams. Team 1 chooses a category and a dollar amount. One person in the class reads the questions under the CATEGORIES column on page 379 aloud. Team 1 has one minute to answer (choose an answer from the Answer Box). If the answer is correct, they "win" the money. If the answer is not correct, Team 2 answers the question to win the money. The team with the most money at the end wins.

EXAMPLE: Team 1: "Animals" for $20.

Reader: What's the most dangerous animal?

Team 1: Mosquitoes (can give you malaria)

$$$	Planets	Animals	Other
$10			
$20			
$30			
$40			
$50			

ANSWER BOX (Choose the answers to the questions from this box.)

Planets	Animals	Other
Pluto	mosquitoes	the Supreme Court
Mercury	the blue whale	the Sahara
Venus	giraffe	the winter solstice
Jupiter	cheetah	(first day of winter)
Mars	race horse	diamond
		Iraq

CATEGORIES

Planets

$10   What is the largest planet in the solar system?
$20   What is the fastest planet?
$30   What is the hottest planet?
$40   What is the farthest planet from the sun?
$50   What is the closest planet to the Earth?

Animals

$10   What is the tallest animal?
$20   What is the most dangerous animal?
$30   What is the fastest land animal?
$40   What is the most valuable animal?
$50   What is the largest and heaviest animal?

Other

$10   What is the hardest gem?
$20   What is the largest desert in the world?
$30   What is the highest court in the United States?
$40   What is the oldest country in the world?
$50   What is the shortest day of the year?

FOCUS 3 >>>>>>>>>>>>>>>> **MEANING/USE**

One Of The + Superlative + Plural Noun

EXAMPLES	EXPLANATION
(a) Bach was **one of the greatest composers** of all time.	*One of the* + superlative + plural noun is common with the superlative form. Example (a) means that there are several composers we think of as the greatest composers of all time. Bach is one of them.
(b) He is **one of the least popular** students in the school.	

Fill in the blanks with *one of the* + superlative + plural noun. Use the words in parentheses.

1. That's ___one of the most expensive cars___ you can buy.
(expensive car)

2. In my opinion, wrestling is _____ you can play. (exciting sport)

3. That was _____ of my life.
(proud moment)

4. That was _____ in the city. (expensive hotel)

5. Drinking and driving is _____ you can do. (bad thing)

6. The chocolate ice cream is _____ on the menu. (good dessert)

7. Dr Jones is _____ in the hospital. (fine doctor)

8. Louis Armstrong was _____ in America. (great jazz musicians)

9. This is _____ in the museum. (beautiful sculpture)

10. Sergei Grinkov, the Olympic ice skater, died in 1995. He was twenty-nine years old. This was _____ in the history of ice skating. (tragic death)

Make sentences with *one of the* + superlative + plural noun. Compare your answers with your classmates'.

EXAMPLE: 1. Prague is one of the most beautiful cities in the world.

1. a beautiful city in the world
2. an interesting place (in the city you are living in)
3. a good restaurant (in the city you are in)
4. a famous leader in the world today
5. a dangerous disease of our time
6. a serious problem in the world
7. a popular food (in the country you come from)
8. a funny show on television

Activities

ACTIVITY 1

Work in a group. Write five questions in the superlative form like the ones in the Opening Task on page 372. Then ask the class the questions.

EXAMPLES: What's the most expensive car in the world?

What is the largest island?

ACTIVITY 2

Write ten questions to ask another student in the class about his or her country or a country he or she knows. Use the superlative form of the words below or add your own.

EXAMPLES: What's the most crowded city in . . . ?

What's the most popular sport in your country?

What's the most unusual food in your city?

crowded city	popular sport	popular food
polluted city	dangerous sport	unusual food
beautiful city	expensive sport	cheap food
important holiday	hot month	important monument
cold month		

ACTIVITY 3

In groups, discuss the following statements. Say if you agree or disagree and why.

1. Money is the most important thing in life.

2. AIDS is the worst disease in the world today.

3. English is the most difficult language to learn.

4. Baseball is the most boring sport.

5. Democracy is the best form of government.

ACTIVITY 4

Interview a partner about his or her life experience. Use the adjectives below to write questions with superlatives. Tell the class about the most interesting things you learned about your partner.

EXAMPLE: What was the best experience you had this year?

What was the most embarrassing moment in your life?

Adjectives to describe experiences:

unusual	sad	exciting
embarrassing	interesting	frightening
happy	dangerous	beautiful
funny	good	bad

ACTIVITY 5

Write a paragraph on one of the topics below:

a. The most embarrassing moment in my life.

b. The most frightening moment in my life.

c. The funniest moment in my life.

ACTIVITY 6

 STEP ❶ Listen to the quiz show. Circle the letter of the correct answer.

Quiz Choices:

1. a. North America   b. Asia   c. Africa

2. a. the elephant   b. the turtle   c. the bear

3. a. New York   b. Los Angeles   c. Chicago

4. a. Chinese   b. French   c. English

5. a. North America   b. Asia   c. Antarctica

6. a. The United States   b. China   c. Canada

7. a. Tokyo   b. Paris   c. Hong Kong

8. a. The Himalayas   b. The Andes   c. The Rockies

9. a. Spain   b. The United States   c. Italy

10. a. Islam/Muslim   b. Christian   c. Hindu

STEP ❷ Discuss your answers with your classmates.

Factual Conditionals

If

That's Life

If you study hard, you get good grades.

Find a match for each statement on the left. Write the letter in the blank next to the number.

1. If you spend more money than you earn, _____
2. If you play with fire, _____
3. If you speak two languages, _____
4. If you don't wash your hands, _____
5. If you care about your health, _____
6. If you eat too much, _____

7. If you respect people, _____
8. If you read a lot, _____
9. If you work hard, _____
10. If you speak well, _____
11. If you study hard, _____

a. you get sick more often.

b. you don't smoke.

c. people respect you.

d. you have money problems.

e. you succeed.

f. you can communicate with more people.

g. people listen to you.

h. you get good grades.

i. you gain weight.

j. you get burned.

k. you learn a lot.

Now make two similar true statements of your own.

12. _____

13. _____

Expressing Facts

Factual conditionals tell about things that are always true and never change.

EXAMPLES		EXPLANATIONS
Clause 1 (If Clause)	**Clause 2 (Main Clause)**	
(a) If you heat water to 212° (degrees) Fahrenheit,	it boils.	Use the simple present in both clauses.
(b) If you water a plant,	it grows.	
(c) When(ever) you mix black and white,	you get gray.	You can use *when* or *whenever* in place of *if*.

EXERCISE 1

Test your knowledge. Circle the correct clause on the right. Discuss your answers with a partner.

1. If you put oil and water together,
   a. the oil stays on top.
   b. they mix.

2. If the temperature outside drops below 32° (degrees) Fahrenheit,
   a. water freezes.
   b. ice melts.

3. If you stay in the sun a lot,
   a. your skin stays young and smooth.
   b. your skin looks old.

4. If you smoke,
   a. you have health problems
   b. you stay in good health.

5. If you don't refrigerate milk,
   a. it stays fresh.
   b. it goes bad.

6. If you fly west,
   a. you gain time.
   b. you lose time.

7. If you fly east,
   a. you gain time.
   b. you lose time.

8. If your body temperature is 103° (degrees) Fahrenheit,
   a. you are well.
   b. you are sick.

Think of the definitions of the words in italics. Find the definitions on the right to complete each statement. Say your statements aloud.

1. If you live in a *democracy*, you
2. If you're *patient*, you don't
3. If you're a *night owl*, you
4. If you're a *teenager*, you
5. If you're a *member of the faculty*, you
6. If you're a *pediatrician*, you
7. If you're a *blue-collar worker*, you may
8. If you're *broke*, you

a. want to be independent.
b. go to bed late.
c. teach in a school or college.
d. lose your temper.
e. work in a factory.
f. don't have any money.
g. treat sick children.
h. vote.

FOCUS 2 >>>>>>>>>>>>>>>>>>>>>> MEANING

Expressing Habitual Relationships

EXAMPLES		EXPLANATIONS
Clause 1 (If Clause)	**Clause 2 (Main Clause)**	
(a) If I **cook**,	my husband **washes** the dishes.	Factual conditionals express present or past habits. Use the same tense in both clauses.
(b) If I **lied**,	my mother **punished** me.	
(c) When(ever) it **snowed**,	we **stayed** home from school.	You can use *when* or *whenever* in place of *if*.

Make sentences with *if, when,* or *whenever* with the words below. Say your sentences aloud and compare your answers.

EXAMPLE: I drive to school/take

If I drive to school, it takes about twenty minutes.

1. I drive to school/take
2. I take the bus to school/take
3. you have elderly parents/worry
4. you live with a roommate/share
5. you buy things on credit/pay
6. you take a vacation every year/feel
7. you never take a vacation/feel
8. you don't own a car/use
9. someone sneezes/say
10. I don't want to cook/eat

In some cultures, people say, "If you go out with wet hair, you get sick." We call these kinds of statements "old wives' tales." They are not always true, but people believe them and repeat them. Read the following "old wives' tales" and decide in your group if they are true or not.

1. If you go out with wet hair, you catch a cold.
2. If your ears are ringing, someone is talking about you.
3. If you eat chicken soup, your cold gets better.
4. If you hold your breath, your hiccups go away.
5. If you eat spinach, you get big and strong.

Now add a few old wives' tales from your country and tell your group about them.

Complete the *if* clauses with a statement of your own.

EXAMPLE: If I feel very tired when I come home, <u>I take a nap for ten minutes</u>.

1. If I don't get my regular sleep, _____.

2. If I get angry, _____.

3. If I get a headache, _____.

4. If I am late, _____.

5. If I gain weight, _____.

6. If I fail an exam, _____.

7. If I have money to spend, _____.

8. If I can't sleep at night, _____.

9. If I eat too much, _____.

10. If I get very worried, _____.

Work with a partner. Ask each other questions about your childhood.

EXAMPLE: When you were a child, what happened if/when you . . . (and told a lie)

If I told a lie, my mother yelled at me.

1. told a lie

2. got sick

3. disobeyed your parents

4. did well in school

5. got a bad grade on your report card

6. came home very late

7. had a serious personal problem

8. fought with your brother or sister

FOCUS 3 >>>>>>>>>>>>>>>>>>>>>> FORM/USE

Order of Clauses in Factual Conditionals

EXAMPLES	EXPLANATIONS
(a) If you study hard, you get good grades.	The *if* clause is usually first.
(b) How do you get an A in this class? You get an A **if you do all the work.**	When the *if* clause contains new information, the *if* clause can be second. When it is second, there is no comma between the two clauses.
(c) How do you get the color gray? You get gray **when(ever) you mix black and white.**	With *when* or *whenever*, you can also change the order of the clauses.

EXERCISE 7

Answer the questions below.

EXAMPLE: When do you feel nervous?

I feel nervous if I have many things to do and little time.

I feel nervous whenever I have a test.

1. When do you feel nervous?
2. When do you get a headache?
3. How do you catch a cold?
4. When do you have trouble sleeping?
5. When did your parents punish you?
6. When were your parents pleased with you?
7. When do you listen to music?
8. When do you get angry?
9. When do you feel happy?
10. How do you know if you're in love?

Activities

Psychologists say there are two personality types: A and B. "Type A" people worry, get nervous, and are under stress all the time. "Type B" people are calm and try to enjoy life.

STEP ❶ Which personality type are you? Complete the statements.

1. Whenever there is a change in my life, I . . .
2. If I have a test, I . . .
3. When I get stuck in traffic, I . . .
4. When I enter a room with people I don't know, I . . .
5. When another driver on the road makes a mistake, I . . .
6. If a friend hurts my feelings, I . . .
7. If I don't hear from my family and friends, I . . .
8. When I have a lot of things to do in one day, I . . .
9. When I don't succeed at something, I . . .
10. When someone criticizes me, I . . .

STEP ❷ Discuss your results in your group. Decide which students in the group are "Type A" personalities and which are "Type B." Explain why. Fill in the chart below.

Name	Type A Personality	Type B Personality
Stefan. If he has a test, he worries a lot.	✔	

ACTIVITY 2

Do you have any special problems or unusual habits? Write down any habits you have. Share your statements with your group. Try to find the person with the most unusual habits.

EXAMPLES: If I eat chocolate, I get a headache.

If I drink more than three cups of coffee a day, I can't sleep.

ACTIVITY 3

Think about your childhood. Make five sentences with *if* clauses about past habits in your childhood.

EXAMPLES: If my sister hit me, I hit her back.

If my mother yelled at me, I felt miserable.

ACTIVITY 4

STEP ❶ Compare habits in different countries. Write the name of a country and complete each *if/when(ever)* clause.

EXAMPLE: In the United States, when you have dinner in a restaurant, you leave a tip.

Country	If/When(ever) Clause 1	Clause 2
United States	you have dinner in a restaurant	Tip
	someone gives you a compliment	
	someone gives you a gift	
	you greet an old friend	
	a baby is born	
	someone sneezes	
	someone invites you to dinner	
	you want to refuse someone's invitation	

STEP ❷ Add two more habits to the list and make sentences about them.

Marcia and Eduardo are having a conversation about what they do if they can't sleep.

 STEP ❶ Listen to the conversation and then check the box if the statements below are true or false.

Read the statements. Check True or False.

	True	False
1. If Eduardo can't sleep, he takes a sleeping pill.		
2. If Marcia can't sleep, she drinks a glass of milk.		
3. If Eduardo can't sleep, he reads a boring book.		
4. If Eduardo drinks milk in the evening, he feels sick.		
5. If Marcia reads a boring book, she falls asleep.		

STEP ❷ What conditions make people have problems with sleep? Tell the class.

STEP ❸ Write three things you do if you can't sleep. Then share your ideas with your classmates. What is the thing people do most?

Appendices

APPENDIX 1   FORMING VERB TENSES

Appendix 1A   Be: Present Tense

I	am	
He She It	is	from Japan.
We You They	are	
There	is	a student from Japan.
There	are	students from all over the world in this class.

Appendix 1B   Be: Past Tense

I He She It	was	happy.
We You They	were	
There	was	a party yesterday.
There	were	a lot of people there.

Appendix 1C   Simple Present

I You We They	work.
He She It	works.

Appendix 1D   Present Progressive

I	am	
He She It	is	working.
We You They	are	

Appendix 1E   Simple Past

I He She It We You They	worked	yesterday.

Appendix 1F   Future Tense with *Will*

I He She It We You They	will work	tomorrow.

Appendix 1G   Future Tense with *Be Going To*

I	am	
He She It	is	going to work in a few minutes.
We You They	are	

Appendix 1H   *Can/Might/May*

I He She It We You They	can might may	work.

Appendix 1I   *Be Able To*

I	am	
He She It	is	able to dance.
We You They	are	

Appendix 2A Plural Nouns

Nouns	Singular	Plural
Regular	book	books
	table	tables
Ends in vowel + *y*	toy	toys
Ends in vowel + *o*	radio	radios
Ends in consonant + *o*	potato	potatoes
	tomato	tomatoes
Ends in -*y*	city	cities
Ends in *f*, *fe*	thief	thieves
	wife	wives
(Except)	chief	chiefs
	chef	chefs
Ends in *ss*, *ch*, *sh*, *x*, and *z*	class	classes
	sandwich	sandwiches
	dish	dishes
	box	boxes
Irregular plural nouns	man	men
	woman	women
	child	children
	person	people
	foot	feet
	tooth	teeth
	mouse	mice
Plurals that stay the same	sheep	sheep
	deer	deer
	fish	fish
No singular form		scissors
		pants
		shorts
		pajamas
		glasses
		clothes

Appendix 2B   Simple Present: Third Person Singular

Rule	Example
1. Add -s to form the third person singular of most verbs.	My brother **sleeps** 8 hours a night
2. Add -es to verbs ending in *sh, ch, x, z,* or *ss.*	She **watches** television every evening.
3. When the verb ends in a consonant + *y*, change the *y* to *i* and add -es.	He **hurries** to class every morning.
4. When the verb ends in a vowel + *y*, do not change the *y*. Add -s.	My sister **plays** the violin.
5. Irregular Forms: have go do	 He **has** a good job. He **goes** to work every day. He **does** the laundry.

Appendix 2C   Present Progressive

Rule		
1. Add -*ing* to the base form of the verb.	talk study do agree	talking studying doing agreeing
2. If the verb ends in a single -*e*, drop the -*e* and add -*ing*.	drive	driving
3. If a one-syllable verb ends in a consonant, a vowel, and a consonant (c-v-c), double the last consonant and add -*ing*.	(c-v-c) s i t r u n	 sitting running
Do not double the consonant, if the verb ends in *w, x,* or *y*.	s h o w f i x p l a y	showing fixing playing
4. In two-syllable verbs that end in a consonant, a vowel, and a consonant (c-v-c), double the last consonant only if the last syllable is stressed.	beGIN LISten	beginning listening
5. If the verb ends in -*ie*, drop the -*ie*, add -*y* and -*ing*.	lie die	lying dying

Appendix 2D   Simple Past of Regular Verbs

1. Add -ed to most regular verbs.	start	started
2. If the verb ends in an -e, add -d.	like	liked
3. If the verb ends in a consonant + y, change the y to i and add -ed.	study	studied
4. If the verb ends in a vowel + y, don't change the y to i. Add -ed.	enjoy play	enjoyed played
5. If a one-syllable verb ends in a consonant, a vowel, and a consonant (c-v-c), double the last consonant and add -ed.	stop	stopped
Do not double the last consonant if it is w, x, or y.	show fix play	showed fixed played
6. If a two-syllable word ends in a consonant, a vowel, and a consonant (c-v-c), double the last consonant if the stress is on the last syllable.	ocCUR LISten	occurred listened

APPENDIX 3 PRONUNCIATION RULES

Appendix 3A   Regular Plural Nouns

/s/	/z/		/ɪz/
After voiceless sounds (f, k, p, t, th)	After voiced sounds (b, d, g, l, m, n, r, v, ng, and vowel sounds)		After s, z, sh, ch, ge/dge sounds. (This adds another syllable to the word.)
cuffs	jobs	pens	classes
books	beds	cars	exercises
maps	rugs	leaves	dishes
pots	schools	rings	sandwiches
months	rooms	days	colleges

Appendix 3B   Simple Present Tense: Third Person Singular

/s/	/z/	/ɪz/
After voiceless sounds (*p, t, f, k*)	After voiced final sounds (*b, d, v, g, l, m, n, r, ng*)	Verbs ending in sh, ch, x, z, ss. (This adds another syllable to the word.)
He sleeps. She works.	She drives a car. He prepares dinner.	He teaches English She rushes to class.

Appendix 3C   Simple Past Tense of Regular Verbs

/t/	/d/	/ɪd/
After voiceless sounds (*s, k, p, f, sh, ch, x*)	After voiced final sounds (*b, g, l, m, n, r, v, x*)	Verbs ending in *t* or *d*. (This adds another syllable to the word.)
He kissed her once. She asked a question.	We learned a song. They waved goodbye.	She painted a picture. The plane landed safely.

APPENDIX 4   TIME EXPRESSIONS

Appendix 4A   Simple Present

Adverbs of Frequency	Frequency Expressions	Time Expressions
always often frequently usually sometimes seldom rarely never	every { morning afternoon night summer winter spring fall day week year } all the time once a week twice a month 3 times a year once in a while	in { 1997 October the fall } on { Monday Sundays January 1st the weekend } at { 6:00 noon night midnight }

Appendix 4B   Present Progressive

now	this semester
right now	this evening
at the moment	this week
today	this year
these days	

Appendix 4C   Past

yesterday	last	ago	in/on/at
yesterday { morning, afternoon, evening }	last { night, week, month, year, summer }	{ an hour, two days, 6 months, a year } ago	in { 1988, June, the evening } on { Sunday, December 1, weekends } at { 6:00, night, midnight }

Appendix 4D   Future

this	next	tomorrow	other	in/on/at
this { morning, afternoon, evening }	next { week, month, year, Sunday, weekend, summer }	tomorrow { morning, afternoon, evening, night }	soon, later, a week from today, tonight, for 3 days, until 3:00	in { 15 minutes, a few days, 2 weeks, March, 2005 } on { Tuesday, May 21 } at { 4:00, midnight }

Appendix 5A   Subject Pronouns

Subject Pronouns		
I	am	
You	are	
He		
She	is	
It		happy.
We		
You	are	
They		

Appendix 5B   Object Pronouns

		Object Pronouns
		me.
		you
		him.
		her.
She	loves	it.
		us.
		you.
		them.

Appendix 5C   Demonstrative Pronouns

This	is a list of subject pronouns.
That	
These	are object pronouns.
Those	

Appendix 5D   Possessive Pronouns

This book is	mine.
	his.
	hers.
	*
	ours.
	yours.
	theirs.

*"It" does not have a possessive pronoun.

Appendix 5E   Reflexive Pronouns

I		myself.
		yourself.
We	love	ourselves.
You		yourselves.
They		themselves.
He		himself.
She	loves	herself.
It		itself.

Appendix 5F   Reciprocal Pronoun

Friends help each other.

Appendix 6A   Possessive Nouns

Bob's Thomas' Thomas's The teacher's The students' The children's Bob and Andrea's	house is big.

Appendix 6B   Possessive Determiners

My Your His Her Its Our Your Their	house is big.

Appendix 6C   Possessive Pronouns

The house is	mine. your. his. hers. * ours. yours theirs.

*"It" does not have a possessive pronoun.

COMPARISONS WITH
APPENDIX 7 — ADJECTIVES AND ADVERBS

Appendix 7A — Comparative Form (to compare two people, places, or things)

Betsy	is	older bigger busier later more punctual less talkative	than	Judy.
	plays the violin	faster more beautifully better		

Appendix 7B — Superlative Form (to compare one thing or person to all the others in a group)

Betsy	is	the oldest the biggest the busiest the most practical the least punctual	of all her sisters.
	plays the violin	the fastest the most beautifully the best	

Appendix 7C — A/As (to say that two people, places, or things are the same)

Betsy	is	as	old big busy practical punctual	as	Judy.
	plays the violin		fast beautifully well		

PAST-TENSE FORMS OF
COMMON IRREGULAR VERBS

Simple Form	Past-Tense Form	Past Participle	Simple Form	Past-Tense Form	Past Participle
be	was	were	leave	left	left
become	became	became	lend	lent	lent
begin	began	begun	let	let	let
bend	bent	bent	lose	lost	lost
bite	bit	bit	make	made	made
blow	blew	blown	meet	met	met
break	broke	broken	pay	paid	]aid
bring	brought	brought	put	put	put
build	built	built	quit	quit	quit
buy	bought	bought	read	read*	read
catch	caught	caught	ride	rode	ridden
choose	chose	chosen	ring	rang	rung
come	came	come	run	ran	run
cost	cost	cost	say	said	said
cut	cut	cut	see	saw	seen
dig	dug	dug	sell	sold	sold
do	did	done	send	sent	sent
draw	drew	drown	shake	shook	shaken
drink	drank	drunk	shoot	shot	shot
drive	drove	driven	shut	shut	shut
eat	ate	eaten	sing	sang	sung
fall	fell	fallen	sit	sat	sat
feed	fed	fed	sleep	slept	slept
feel	felt	felt	speak	spoke	spoken
fight	fought	fought	spend	spent	spent
find	found	found	stand	stood	stood
fly	flew	flown	steal	stole	stolen
forget	forgot	forgotten	swim	swam	swum
get	got	gotten	take	took	taken
give	gave	given	teach	taught	taught
go	went	gone	tear	tore	torn
grow	grew	grown	tell	told	told
hang	hung	hung	think	thought	thought
have	had	had	throw	threw	thrown
hear	heard	heard	understand	understood	understood
hide	hid	hidden	wake	woke	woken
hit	hit	hit	wear	wore	worn
hold	held	held	win	won	won
hurt	hurt	hurt	write	wrote	written
keep	kept	kept			
know	knew	known			
lead	led	led			

* Pronounce the base form: /rid/; pronounce the past-tense form: rɛd.

Answer Key
(for puzzles and problems only)

Answers to Opening Task (page 257)

1. Martin Luther King, Jr. wasn't African;, he was African-American. He was a civil rights leader.

2. The Beatles were British. They weren't hairdressers; they were musicians.

3. Marilyn Monroe was American. She was an actress.

4. Indira Gandhi was Indian. She wasn't a rock singer; she was the prime minister of India.

5. Pierre and Marie Curie were French. They weren't fashion designers; they were scientists.

6. Mao was Chinese. He was a political leader in the People's Republic of China.

7. Jacqueline Kennedy Onassis wasn't Greek; she was American. She was the wife of John F. Kennedy, president of the United States, and later of Aristotle Onassis, who was a Greek millionaire.

8. George Washington, Thomas Jefferson, Abraham Lincoln and Theodore Roosevelt weren't Canadian, they were American. They were presidents. Their heads are on Mt. Rushmore in South Dakota.

Answer to Activity 1 (page 301)

The prisoner stood on a block of ice with the rope around his neck. When the ice melted, his feet didn't touch the ground, so he hanged himself.

Exercises
(second parts)

Exercise 6 (page 21)

Chart B

Name: Age:	Cindy 22	Shelley 27	Gloria 30
1. Height			
tall			
average height		✔	
short			
2. Weight			
thin	✔		
average weight			
overweight			✔
3. Personality			
shy		✔	
friendly			
quiet		✔	
talkative			
neat		✔	✔
messy			
funny			
serious		✔	✔
nervous			
calm		✔	

Answers to Exercise 6 (page 36)

MAP B

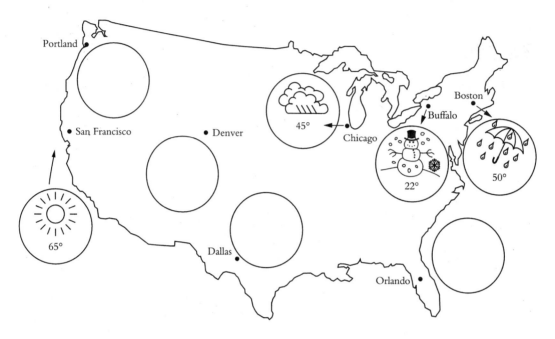

Exercise 10 (page 42)

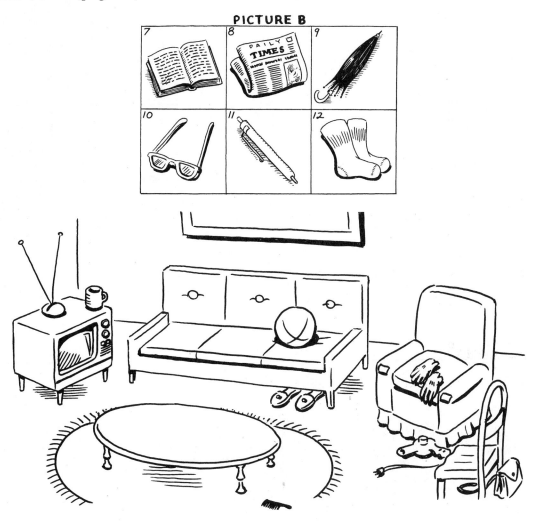

PICTURE B

Exercise 2 (page 132)

Student B:

	Nahal		Sang-Woo	
	Yes	**No**	**Yes**	**No**
1. like to learn English			✔	
2. want to meet English-speaking people	✔			
3. feel nervous when speaking English			✔	
4. like to work in groups	✔			
5. need grammar rules to learn English			✔	
6. learn by speaking and listening to English	✔			
7. learn by reading and writing English			✔	
8. learn slowly, step by step		✔		
9. try new ways of learning				✔

Conclusion to Exercise 12 (page 286)

Answers to Exercise 15 (page 289)

Text B

1. Doina grew up in _____ (where).

2. She married a government official.

3. She had _____ in 1976 (what).

4. Doina was unhappy _____ (why).

5. She thought of ways to escape.

6. She taught her daughter _____ (what).

7. On October 9, 1988, she and her daughter swam across the Danube River to Serbia.

8. _____ caught them (who).

9. Doina and her daughter went to jail.

10. They tried to escape _____ (when).

11. Finally, they left Romania on foot in the middle of the night.

12. They flew to _____ in 1989 (where).

13. Doina went to school to learn English.

14. She wrote _____ (what) in her ESL class.

Activity 6 (page 292)

Only the Host looks at this game board.

GAME BOARD

$$$	Category 1 PEOPLE	Category 2 WH-QUESTIONS	Category 3 YES/NO QUESTIONS
$10	Ms. Dito.	A VCR.	Yes, she did.
$20	Harry.	On the first day of classes.	Yes, he did.
$30	The Director.	In the language lab.	No, he didn't.
$40	Professor Brown.	Because he needed pay for the ESL classes again this semester.	No, he didn't.
$50	The students.	She noticed grammar mistakes in the note.	Yes, they did.

Exercise 4 (page 377)

CHART B

	North America	South America	Asia	Europe	Africa	The World
long river	The Mississippi		The Yangtze		The Nile	
large country		Brazil		France		The People's Republic of China
populated country	The United States		The People's Republic of China		Nigeria	
high mountain		Mt. Aconcagua		Mt. Elbrus		Mt. Everest
small country	Bermuda		Macao		the Seychelles	

Credits

Text Credits

Unit 8, Exercise 4: Cartoon by Sergio Aragones, from *Mad Magazine*. Reprinted by permission of Sergio Aragones.

Unit 18, Exercise 3: Cartoon by Sergio Aragones, from *Mad Magazine*. Reprinted by permission of Sergio Aragones.

Unit 18, Exercise 12, and Activity 2: Cartoon by Sergio Aragones, from *Mad Magazine*. Reprinted by permission of Sergio Aragones.

Photo Credits

Page 1: © Rob Crandall, The Image Works. Page 5: seated couple, © D. Young-Wolf, Photo Edit; student, © Michelle Bridwell, Photo Edit. Page 6: Argentinian students, © Michael Dwyer, Stock Boston; Nigerian men, © Beryl Goldberg. Page 29: Pyramids, The Bettmann Archive; Himalayan Mountains, Mark Antman, The Image Works; Fourth of July fireworks, © Archive Photos/Lambert; the Kremlin, © Bill Aaron, Photo Edit. Page 91: © Dana White, Photo Edit. Page 257: all photos, © Archive Photos. Page 258: all photos, © Archive Photos. Page 266: The Image Works. Page 303: © Archive Photos/Curry. Page 392: © Reuters/Jack Naegelen Archive Photos.

Index

A/an, 102
   with singular count nouns, 49, 50, 59, 102, 163
   using *a* vs. *an*, 50, 62
Ability, verbs expressing, 206, 211
Above, 40
Across, 156
Actions, adverbs to talk about, 184
Actions in progress, present progressive for, 227
Adjective(s)
   be plus, 19
   comparative, 341–56
      as . . . as to express similarities/differences,
         350
      form of, 343–44
      irregular, 344
      polite comparisons, 351
      questions with, 348
   with *-ly* ending, 180
   to talk about person, place or thing, 184
   very before, to make stronger, 19, 62
Adjective phrases, 239–56
   with *another*, 247
   form/meaning of, 241
   intensifiers, 250
   with *other/other(s)/the other(s)*, 247
   questions with *which one/ones*, 245
Adverbs
   comparative, 357–70
      expressing similarities and differences, 361
      form/use of, 359
      questions with *how*, 364
   of frequency, 135, 359
      position of, 137
   irregular, 180
   of manner, 177–86
      form/meaning of, 179
      spelling of, 180
      talking about verb or action with, 184
Advice, imperatives to give, 151
A few/few, 168
Affirmative imperatives, 149
Affirmative statements
   be going to in, 310
   be in, 3
      past tense of, 259
   can in, 206
   have in, 65
   irregular past-tense verbs in, 277–79
   may/might in, 320

   present progressive tense in, 221–22
      affirmative contractions, 222
   quantifiers in, 164
   simple present in, 111
   some in, 73
   will in, 306
A little/little, 168
All in frequency expressions, 116, 117
Almost always, meaning of, 135
Along, 156
Always
   meaning of, 135
   position of, 137
And, as sentence connector, 214
Another, 247
Any, *have* with, 73
Apostrophe-*s*/apostrophe for possessive nouns, 85
Around, 156
Articles
   the, 102, 374
   a/an, 102
      with singular count nouns, 49, 50, 59, 102, 163
      using *a* vs. *an*, 50, 62
As . . . as to show similarities, 350, 361
At
   as preposition of time, 315
   in time expressions, 116, 117
At the moment, 221
Auxiliary verbs after *than* in comparative adverb,
   359
Away from, 154

Be, 1–46
   in affirmative statements, 3
   contractions of, 9, 23
      negative, 17, 23, 261
      plus *not*, 23, 225
      in present progressive, 222
   in introductions and greetings, 11–12
   in negative statements, 23
   past tense of, 257–68
      in affirmative sentences, 259
      in negative statements, 261
      in *wh*-questions, 265
      in *yes/no* questions and short answers, 263
   plus adjective, 19
   plus adjective and noun, 62
   prepositions of location after, 40–41
   subject pronouns with, 5

contraction of, 9, 23
there plus, 95. *See also There is/there are*
using *it* with
  to talk about time, 37–38
  to talk about weather, 35
wh-question words with, 31, 265
  to ask questions about English, 34
in *yes/no* questions and short answers, 17, 263
Be *able to*, 211
Be *going to*
  for making predictions about future, 305,
    310–11
  to talk about future intentions or plans, 318
Behind, 40
Between, 40
Body parts, possessive determiners with, 88
But, 214
By plus reflexive pronouns, 296

Can
  form/meaning of, 206, 211
  questions with, 208
    asking for help with English, 210
Can't/cannot, 206
Clauses in factual conditionals, order of, 391
Comma
  after frequency and time expressions at begin-
    ning of sentence, 117
  before sentence connector, 214
  after time expression at beginning of sentence,
    281, 314
Comparative adjectives, 341–56
  as . . . as to express similarities/differences, 350
  form of, 343–44
  irregular, 344
  polite comparisons, 351
  questions with, 348
  regular, 343–44
Comparative adverbs, 357–70
  expressing similarities and differences, 361
  form/use of, 359
  questions with *how*, 364
Conditionals, factual, 385–94
  to express facts, 387
  to express habitual relationships, 388
  order of clauses in, 391
Connectors, sentence, 214
Containers, measure words for, 171
Contraction(s)
  in affirmative present progressive, 222
  with *be*, 9, 23
    negative, 17, 23, 261
    in past tense, 261
    plus *not*, 23, 225

in present progressive, 222
of *cannot* (*can't*), 206
of *it is* (*it's*), 88
negative, with *have*, 68
in negative present progressive, 225
of *there is* (*there's*), 96
of *who is* (*who's*), 90
Count nouns, 49, 59
  a/an with singular, 49, 50, 59, 102, 163
  any with plural, 73
  how many with, 163, 169
  measure words with, 171
  noncount words compared to, 49, 59–60
  quantifiers with, 164
  regular plural, 49, 59
    pronunciation of final *-s* and *-es*, 56
    spelling of, 54
  review of, 163
  there is/there are with, 96
    there isn't/there aren't/there's no, 98
    yes/no questions with, 100

Definite articles, 102
Demonstratives, 81–84
  asking what things are with, 83
  form and meaning of, 81
  yes/no questions with, 83
Description of people, using *have* in, 76
Determiners, possessive, 88
Did in past tense *yes/no* questions and short
  answers, 284
Did not/didn't in past tense negative statements,
  283
  negative answers, 284
Differences
  not as . . . as to show, 350, 361
  for polite comparisons, 351
Direction(s)
  giving, 157–58
    imperatives for, 151
  prepositions of, 154–57
Direct object, 189
  pronoun as, 193
  with separable vs. inseparable phrasal verbs,
    330
Dr., in greetings, 12
Do/does
  in affirmative and negative short answers, 70
  irregular forms in simple present, 113
  after *than* in comparative adverb, 359
  in *yes/no* questions
    with *have*, 69
    in simple present, 131
Down, 156

Each other, 298
Emotions, nonprogressive verbs of, 229
Emphasis, position of new information for, 197
English, getting information about
   questions for, 34, 143, 210
   in simple present, 143
Every in frequency expressions, 116, 117

Factual conditionals, 385–94
   to express facts, 387
   to express habitual relationships, 388
   order of clauses in, 391
Fairly, as intensifier, 250
Feelings, nonprogressive verbs of, 229
Few/a few, 168
For
   in future time expression, 315
   indirect object following, 193
     verbs that do not omit *for*, 200
Frequency, adverbs of, 135
   comparative, 359
   position of, 137
Frequency expressions, 116, 117
Future time, 303–24
   making predictions about, 305–11
     be going to for, 305, 310–11
     will for, 305, 306–7
     may/might for possibility in, 320
   talking about future intentions or plans, 318
   time expressions for, 314–15

Go, irregular forms in simple present, 113
"Gonna," 311
Greetings, verb be in, 11–12

Habits, simple present for, 111, 227
Habitual relationships, factual conditionals to
   express, 388
Hardly, 180
Have, 65–78
   in affirmative statements, 65
   asking for something politely, 75
   to describe people, 76
   irregular forms in simple present, 113
   meaning of, 67
   in negative statements, 68
   with *some/any*, 73
   in *yes/no* questions and short answers, 69–70
Her/hers, 88
Herself, 295
Himself, 295
His, 88
How
   with *be*, 31

   questions with, 364
     in simple present, 139
How many/how much, 169
   questions with, 163
How much is/how much are, 61
How often, questions in simple present with, 139
How old with be, 31

If in factual conditionals, 387, 388, 391
Imperatives, 149–54
   affirmative, 149
   negative, 149
   polite, 149
   uses of, 150–51
     appropriate, 153
In
   as preposition of location, 40
   as preposition of time, 315
   in time expressions, 116, 117
In back of, 40
Indefinite articles, 102
Indirect object pronouns, 193
Indirect objects, 193
   position of, 195–96
   verbs that do not omit *to/for* with, 200
Infinitives after *like/want/need*, 122
In front of, 40
Inseparable phrasal verbs, 330, 334
Instructions, imperatives to give, 151
Intensifiers, 250
Intentions or plans, talking about future, 318
In(to), 154, 155
Introductions, verb be in, 11–12
Irregular adverbs, 180
   comparative, 359
Irregular comparative adjectives, 344
Irregular plural nouns, 58
   apostrophe-*s* for possessive, 85
Irregular superlatives, 375
Irregular verbs, past tense, 277–79
Its
   it's vs., 88
   as possessive determiner, 88
Itself, 295
It with *be*
   to talk about time, 37–38
   to talk about weather, 35

Know how to, 211

Least, superlatives with, 374
Less
   with comparative adjectives, 343–44
   with comparative adverbs, 359

Like, form and meaning of, 122
Little/a little, 168
Location, prepositions of, 40–41

Manner, adverbs of, 177–86
    form/meaning of, 179
    spelling of, 180
    talking about verb or action with, 184
May/might, 320
Meaning of word, questions to ask about, 143
Measure words, 171
Mental states, nonprogressive verbs of, 229
Mine, as possessive pronoun, 88
Mr./Ms./Miss, in greetings, 12
More
    with comparative adjectives, 343–44
    with comparative adverbs, 359
Most, superlatives with, 374
Much, for stronger comparative adjectives, 344
My, as possessive determiner, 88
Myself, 295

Near, as preposition of location, 40
Need, form and meaning of, 122
Negative contractions
    with *be*, 17, 23, 261
    with *have*, 68
Negative imperatives, 149
Negative statements
    any in, 73
    be going to in, 310
    be in, 23
        past tense of, 261
    cannot in, 206
    have in, 68
    may/might in, 320
    past tense in, 283
    present progressive tense in, 225
    quantifiers in, 164
    simple present in, 119
    there isn't/there aren't/there's no, 98
    will in, 306
Never, meaning of, 135
New information in sentence, position of, 197
Next to, 40
Noncount nouns, 49, 59–60
    any with plural, 73
    how much with, 163, 169
    quantifiers with, 164
    review of, 163
    there is/there are with, 96
        in negative statements, 98
        there isn't/there aren't/there's no, 98
        yes/no questions with, 100

Nonprogressive (stative) verbs, 229
Not
    contraction of *be* followed by, 23, 225
    in negative present progressive statements, 225
Not as . . . as, to show differences, 350, 361
Not much/not many, 168
Nouns, 47–64. *See also* Count nouns; Noncount nouns
    articles with. *See* Articles
    be plus adjective plus, 62
    as direct object with separable vs. inseparable phrasal verb, 330
    irregular plural, 58, 85
    multiple, subject-verb agreement with, 96
    possessive, 85
    regular plural
        pronunciation of final *-s* and *-es*, 56
        spelling of, 54
Now, with present progressive, 221

Object pronouns, 190
    indirect, 193
    after *than* in comparative adverb, 359
Objects
    direct, 189
        pronoun as, 193
        with separable vs. inseparable phrasal verbs, 330
    indirect, 193
        position of, 195–96
        verbs that do no omit *to/for* with, 200
        phrasal verbs without, 336
        position of new information in sentence, 197
Offers, imperatives to make, 151
Off (of), 154, 155
Often/frequently
    meaning of, 135
    position of, 137
On
    as preposition of location, 40
    as preposition of time, 315
    in time expressions, 116, 117
Once in frequency expressions, 116, 117
One of the plus superlative plus plural nouns, 380
One/ones
    adjective phrases after, 245
    substituted for nouns, to avoid repetition, 245
On(to), 154, 155
Opposite, 40
Or, as sentence connector, 214
Orders, imperatives to give, 151
Other/other(s)/the other(s), 247
Our/ours, 88
Ourselves, 295

Out of, 154, 155
Over, 156

Particles in phrasal verbs, 327, 328
   separable vs. inseparable, 330
Past, 156
Past tense, 269–90
   of *be*, 257–68
      in affirmative sentences, 259
      in negative statements, 261
      in *wh*-questions, 265
      in *yes/no* questions and short answers, 263
   irregular verbs in, 277–79
   in negative statements, 283
   pronunciation of *-ed* ending, 274
   spelling of regular verbs in, 271–72
   time expressions in, 281
   in *wh*-questions, 286–87
   in *yes/no* sentences and short answers, 284
People, *have* to describe, 76
Phrasal verbs, 325–40
   form of, 327
   meaning of, 327, 328
   without objects, common, 336
   separable and inseparable, 330
      common, 332–34
Please, in polite imperatives, 149
Plural nouns
   any with, 73
   irregular, 58, 85
   regular
      pronunciation of final *-s* and *-es*, 56
      spelling of, 54
Politeness
   asking for something politely with *have*, 75
   polite comparisons, 351
   polite imperatives, 149
Portions, measure words for, 171
Possession, nonprogressive verbs of, 229
Possessive determiners, 88
Possessive nouns, 85
Possessive pronouns, 88
Possessive questions with *whose*, 83, 90
Possibility, *may/might* to show future, 320
Prepositional phrase, 41
   after superlatives, 373
Prepositions
   of direction, 154–57
   of location, 40–41
   of time, to talk about future time, 315
Present progressive tense, 219–38
   in affirmative statements, 221–22
      affirmative contractions, 222
   choosing simple present vs., 227

   in negative statements, 225
   spelling of verbs ending in *-ing*, 223
   verbs not usually used in, 229
   in *wh*-questions, 234
   in *yes/no* questions and short answers, 232
Pretty, as intensifier, 250
Prices, asking questions about, 61
Professor, in greetings, 12
Pronouns
   as direct object with separable vs. inseparable
      phrasal verb, 330
   object, 190, 359
      indirect, 193
   possessive, 88
   reciprocal, 298
   reflexive, 295, 296
   subject, 5, 9, 23
   after *than* in comparative adverb, 359
Pronunciation
   of *-ed* ending, 274
   of final *-s* and *-es* in regular plural nouns, 56
   questions to ask about, 143
   third person singular simple present tense, 113
   voiceless and voiced sounds, 113, 274

Quantifiers, 161–76
   a few/few and *a little/little*, 168
   form and meaning of, 164
   measure words, 171
   questions with *how many* and *how much*, 163, 169
Quantities, measure words for specific, 171
Questions. *See also* Wh-questions; Yes/no questions
   and short answers
   any in, 73
   asking for something politely, 75
   asking what things are, with demonstratives, 83
   with *can*, 208
   with comparative adjectives, 348
   for getting information about English, 34, 143,
      210
   with *how*, 364
   with *how many* and *how much*, 163, 169
   with *how much is/how much are*, 61
   with *which one/ones*, 245
   about *whose*, 83, 90
Quite, as intensifier, 250

Rather, as intensifier, 250
Reciprocal pronouns, 298
Reflexive pronouns, 295, 296
Requests, imperatives to make, 151
Right now, with present progressive, 221
Routines, simple present for talking about, 111

Seldom/rarely, meaning of, 135
Senses, nonprogressive verbs of, 229
Sentence connectors, 214
Separable phrasal verbs, 330
    common, 332–33
Short answers. *See* Yes/no questions and short answers
Similarities, *as . . . as* to show, 350, 361
Simple past tense. *See* Past tense
Simple present tense, 109–46
    with adverbs of frequency, 135
        position of, 137
    in affirmative statements, 111
    choosing present progressive vs., 227
    in factual conditionals, 387
    frequency and time expressions in, 116, 117, 227
    getting information about English in, 143
    like/want/need, 122
    in negative statements, 119
    talking about habits and routines with, 111, 227
    talking about things that are always true with, 120, 227
    third person singular spelling and pronunciation, 113
    wh-questions in, 139
        with *who/whom*, 139, 141
    yes/no questions in, 131
So, as sentence connector, 214
Some
    a few and *a little* meaning, 168
    have with, 73
Sometimes
    meaning of, 135
    position of, 137
Spelling
    of adverbs of manner, 180
    questions to ask about, 143
    of regular past tense verbs, 271–72
    of regular plural count nouns, 54
    third person singular simple present tense, 113
    of verbs ending in *-ing*, 223
Stative (nonprogressive) verbs, 229
Subject pronoun
    with *be*, 3
        contraction of, 9, 23
    after *than* in comparative adverb, 359
Subjects, multiple or with hyphens, apostrophe-*s* at end of, 85
Subject-verb agreement, 241
    with multiple nouns, 96
Suggestions, imperatives to make, 151
Superlatives, 371–84
    irregular forms of, 375
    meaning of, 373

one of the plus superlative plus plural nouns, 380
    regular forms of, 374

Temporary actions, present progressive for, 227
Than
    with comparative adjectives, 343–44
    with comparative adverbs, 359
That/those
    asking what things are with, 83
    form and meaning of, 81
    yes/no questions with, 83
The, 102
    plus superlative, 374
Their/theirs, 88
Themselves, 295
There is/there are, 93–108
    contraction of *there is* (*there's*), 96
    form of, 96
    meaning and use of, 95
    there isn't/there aren't/there's no, 98
    yes/no questions with, 100
They are vs. *there are*, 95
Third person singular in simple present, spelling and pronunciation of, 113
This/these, 81–84
    asking what things are with, 83
    form and meaning of, 81
    yes/no questions with, 83
Through, 156
Time, using *be* to talk about, 37–38
Time expressions
    future, 314–15
    past tense, 281
    with present progressive, 221, 227
    simple present, 227
        form of, 117
        meaning of, 116
Titles in greetings, use of, 12
To
    indirect object following, 193
        verbs that do not omit to, 200
    as preposition of direction, 154
Truths, simple present for, 120, 227
Twice, 116, 117

Under, 40
Until, 315
Up, 156
Usually, 135

Verbs. *See also* Be; Have
    adverbs to talk about, 184
    commonly used with reflexive pronouns/*by* plus reflexive pronouns, 296

ending in *-ing*, spelling of, 223
    expressing ability, 206, 211
    nonprogressive (stative), 229
    not usually used in present progressive, 229
    phrasal. *See* Phrasal verbs
    that do not omit *to/for* with indirect objects, 200
Very, 184
    before adjective to make it stronger, 19, 62
    as intensifier, 250
Voiced/voiceless sounds, 113
    pronunciation of *-ed* ending after, 274

Want, form and meaning of, 122
Warning, imperatives to give, 151
Weather, using *be* to talk about, 35
What
    to ask questions about English, 34
    with *be*, 31
    questions in simple present with, 139
What time
    with *be*, 31
    questions in simple present with, 139
When
    with *be*, 31
    questions in simple present with, 139
When/whenever in factual conditionals, 387, 388, 391
Where
    with *be*, 31
    questions in simple present with, 139
Which one/ones, questions with, 245
Whose
    questions about, 83, 90
    who's vs., 90
Who/whom, questions in simple present with, 139, 141

Who with *be*, 31
Wh-questions
    with *be*, 31
        to ask questions about English, 34
        in past tense, 265
    be going to in, 311
    past tense in, 286–87
    present progressive in, 234
    in simple present, 139
        with *who/whom*, 139, 141
    will in, 307
Why
    with *be*, 31
    questions in simple present with, 139
Will
    for making predictions about future, 305, 306–7
    to talk about future intentions or plans, 318

Yes/no questions and short answers
    be going to in, 310
    be in, 17
        past tense of, 263
    with demonstratives, 83
    have in, 69–70
    may/might not used in, 320
    past tense in, 284
    present progressive in, 232
    in simple present, 131
    with *there is/there are*, 100
    will in, 306
Yourself/yourselves, 295
Your/yours, 88